BUSINESS AS UNUSUAL

THE PEOPLE AND PRINCIPLES AT HERMAN MILLER

BY

HUGH DE PREE

Copyright © 1986 by Hugh D. De Pree

First published in 1986 by Herman Miller, Inc.
8500 Byron Road, Zeeland, Michigan 49464.

Printed in the United States of America.

Library of Congress Cataloging in Publication Data

De Pree, Hugh, 1915-
  Business as unusual

  Includes index.
  1. Herman Miller (Firm) — History.   2. Furniture industry
and trade — United States — History.   I. Title.
HD9773.U7H383   1986   338.7'6841'00973   86-18221
ISBN 0-87911-005-8

To Ruth,
Caring contributor, with love.

CONTENTS

ACKNOWLEDGMENTS

Since June, 1985, William Houseman
has been a most important part of this
project. Bill has come to know and understand the people and principles of
Herman Miller. He has been editor, op-
timist, critic, and resource, interviewing
some thirty people connected to my time
at Herman Miller. He has brought life,
clarity, enrichment, and continuity to
the messages I was trying to frame. Not
since Charles Eames have I worked with
a man who makes such demands for excellence and hard work, who forced me
again and again to think and rethink,
write and rewrite. Our experience together has been a time of fun and frustration, of satisfaction and vexation, and
through this relationship we have become friends.

I was fortunate enough to find four
other people who became committed to
this book: Linda Folland, Steve Fryk-
holm, Clark Malcolm, and Linda Powell.
They made it better than I had ever
thought it might be.

H

erman Miller's headquarters is in Zeeland, Michigan, a tiny town near Grand Rapids where, in the 1950s, cows still grazed in the fields outside the company's factory doors. Zeeland's population, primarily descended from Dutch Reformists whose religious tradition still influences life in the town, continues to make up the nucleus of Herman Miller's work force. That same tradition is apparent in the moral and practical guideposts of the De Pree family, which has led the company since its founding over fifty years ago. In that time, D.J. De Pree, the company's ninety-five-year-old patriarch, and his sons Hugh and Max developed a small, family-owned business into a multi-national, publicly held corporation whose future rests with the men and women who have risen through the ranks of Herman Miller's remarkable Scanlon Plan—a system of employee participation and shareholding that creates intense company loyalty and camaraderie.

How did they do it?

This book does not provide simple answers for those who would follow the Herman Miller example. What it does communicate is the creative spirit that has always characterized the company's management, and the remarkable group of designers and architects responsible for its aesthetic accomplishments.

In an effort to isolate those principles and attitudes that have made Herman Miller significant as an enterprise, Hugh De Pree has put down in these pages his reminiscences of the company's evolution viewed from his particular entrepreneurial perspective—that of a risk-taker but one with a practical business sensibility. Since Hugh's retirement in 1980, his brother Max, now Chairman of Herman Miller, has found new ways to deal with the fantastic growth the company experienced under Hugh's leadership, when the decision was made to manufacture primarily office and health care systems in place of the domestic furniture that had been the company's hallmark. The Action Office and Co/Struc systems were the work of Robert Propst, a gifted innovator.

These systems designs were an emphatic departure from the Herman Miller traditions that were based on the "inevitable rightness" that characterized the work of George Nelson, Charles and Ray Eames and Alexander Girard. Their designs had made the company's reputation when Americans were eager for the material goods denied them through years of depression and war. Nevertheless, the company struggled in the *avant-garde* for decades: first with the works of Gilbert Rohde in the 1930s and after World War II with the brilliant Nelson and Eames, whose lasting contributions to twentieth-century design in America are indisputable.

Over the years, Herman Miller has been a generous, open-minded client of its designers. The company's unwavering trust and belief in their integrity and creativity has built enduring relationships. Through his innate wisdom, D.J. De Pree knew that the George Nelsons and Charles Eameses of this world would not make their homes in Zeeland; so began the practice of working with consulting designers who come in and out of the headquarters town as needed, a system that continues today with such designers as Bill Stumpf and Don Chadwick.

Herman Miller's progress has always been tied to innovation: a willingness to risk and a willingness to fail. This attitude, earlier based on D.J. De Pree's unique ethical system that espoused modern design because it was morally right, has given way to the more sophisticated humanism of a younger generation. With all that, it is important to note that great design has neither period nor stylistic limitations. When we reexamine the Herman Miller furniture of the 1950s in light of today's needs, the best of it looks as "right" today as it did then to the De Prees

FOREWORD

and to the small but dedicated band of modernists of that earlier decade.

Mildred Friedman
Design Curator, Walker Art Center

INTRODUCTION

Hirstory can't be left to fend for itself. Families, nations, communities have histories, traditions, rituals, and customs. So do corporations.

When one marries into a family or immigrates to a nation or moves to a new town, it takes time and study and often passion to join the new tribe. So it is with a corporation.

In the process of getting to know the new tribe, we are likely to ask several very natural questions of our new companions.

What is your name?

Where were you born?

Where do you live?

What do you do?

Why?

Tell me about your family.

What's important in your life?

What do you want to be when you grow up?

To be able to get the answers to these and other questions from one of the tribal elders is very special. For people who care about Herman Miller and wish to be a part of its history, of fulfilling its legacy, this book will be very special. It was written by one of our tribal elders who gave his entire working life to the company, my brother Hugh.

Most people who write about history haven't been part of making it. This book was written by one of the makers, and this history tells us the what and the where and the how of things. Most important, though, this book helps to tell us *why* we are what we are. It tells us the origin of the rituals and traditions and events that make up our legacy. It gives us a chance to understand that vision and wisdom are connected in a curious way to naiveté. Our history is not merely a list of the tangibles of life; rather, it's a compilation of events and happenings, beliefs and commitments, mistakes and successes.

This history is special because it gives us insights into what's most important and, at the same time, most fragile about our future. The message is really quite simple. What counts are the things we believe, our understanding of the importance of people, our commitment to problem solving and good design, a passion for the way in which things ought to be done, an understanding that what's most important is the quality of our relationships. These beliefs and understandings will continue our legacy.

As I said earlier, history cannot be left to fend for itself. Hugh's book expresses our history and gives our history a chance to bequeath to us its lessons and its legacy.

Max De Pree

Some years ago we met with Peter Drucker to discuss problems confronting Herman Miller. Two of the most serious, we felt, were growth and organization.

"How many new people came with Herman Miller last year?" Drucker asked.

We gave him the figure.

"And how many do you plan to add in the next year?"

We gave him our estimate. We anticipated a sizable increase.

Drucker then led us in a discussion of the need to make sure that these new people come to know the company, to understand who we are and what we try to do. He said, "Without this knowledge, growth will be very difficult." He wanted us to make sure that the lore of the company was carried forward to new generations.

What needs to be passed along? The lore certainly: the tribal stories of an organization. And history: the things that happened. Beliefs and principles: the building blocks of an enterprise, without which a whole structure can, and often does, crumble. And the people: all who struggle with the tasks and complexities in the world of business. All of these things must be enduring if a business is to survive and grow.

Once it was normal within a company to remember the roots from which it grew; to know not only what it does but also *who it is;* and to believe the company could make a difference—a contribution to society—and that it was a company goal to make such a difference.

Usually this sense of mission was made clear because one man, or a small group, had personal values and a philosophy about the way a business should operate and were able to build these into the business: Alfred Sloan, Henry Ford, Thomas Watson, John Deere, Walt Disney and Trammell Crow—all of these men, and sometimes their successors, did this. Bill Hewlett and Dave Packard, from a start in one's garage, molded their values into Hewlett-Packard so deeply that even today, with over 80,000 employees, these values still guide the company.

Among companies today, Hewlett-Packard is a rare exception. Corporate attitudes about values and a guiding philosophy have lost their currency. The idea that a company might survive because it has a "being," that it is a "somebody," has eroded badly in recent years. I recall attending a Conference Board meeting fifteen years ago where all but two of the chief executive officers present agreed that business is bottom-line profits—period. "Our business," they said, "is making money." Then and now, management's preoccupation with finance, cash flow, mergers and acquisitions prompts it too easily to ask, "How will this affect me?" Satisfying the investment community grabs management's attention, and the most important goal is to build a glowing financial image to enhance the probability of a merger or acquisition— followed by the escape of a few beneficiaries by golden parachute.

This book describes a journey through business as business can be, not as it is usually conducted. It has been written to carry forward the life and lore of one company. It consists of a series of essays by one person, myself. These essays can be read either separately or as a book. However, I should like to explain that in order to broaden the perspective of this book, I have included many valuable contributions from other people. A series of interviews was conducted with some of my former associates at Herman Miller and others with special knowledge of the company, and you will find their views in these pages. Some have been incorporated in my text, while others appear after some of the essays.

The business model found in these pages is Herman Miller, Inc. As models go, this one is by no means perfect. What this company has done over the years has not always been successful. It has not always been a winner. But it has always tried to operate by certain beliefs and principles, especially the principles of trust, stewardship, equity, and innovation.

Trust, the first principle: Trust is the father of openness, and openness demands a commitment to *letting it happen,* to believing that there is usually someone close to the problem who is able to solve it, or someone close to the opportunity who is able to exploit it. Only the leaders of the organization can make such a commitment. It is they who must be open to ideas, abilities, actions, and the influence and contributions of others.

People are usually anxious to perform and will do more than you expect if they have the information they need, understand the direction and constraints, and believe they have the freedom to fail.

Setting a climate of openness and trust returns to leaders a rewarding sense of satisfaction and joy, for it raises the strong probability that new ideas influencing the direction of the company will occur. So we see that it becomes the leader's responsibility to support talent through openness.

It has been said that trust is a rare privilege but also a heavy burden, for one's integrity is at stake. Certainly, responsibility and accountability rest on the leader; but not the exercise of power, since power changes everyone and all relationships. Power must be focused in ownership, either the shareholder kind of ownership or through those who own the company by virtue of their contributions and the dedication of their lives.

Trust makes it possible to assemble the diverse abilities needed to achieve our potential, using the tensions that may arise to help us see opportunities and solutions more clearly. We may see that a diversity of gifts and opinions can be animated by the same spirit.

We know that fruitful relationships depend on trust, and it is through open, connecting relationships that an organization best functions. From trust develops the sense of a community of working people in which each person's work connects naturally with the next person's, thereby forming a family of accountable contributors.

The difference at Herman Miller is the energy beamed from thousands of unique contributions by people who understand, accept and commit themselves to the idea that they can in fact make a difference. Thus, this difference at Herman Miller is not "the lengthened shadow" of one man, nor is it derived from an elite group of managers.

Stewardship, the second principle: All of us are stewards of our own talents, gifts, experience and knowledge. Even more, a leader is a steward of the talents and resources placed in his care, and consequently for the ideas, products and programs designed and developed by these resources. But there is another dimension to stewardship, nowhere better described than in I Corinthians: "Moreover it is required in stewards that a man be found faithful."

A faithful steward recognizes the potential in those things for which he is accountable and employs them to ensure appropriate benefits for society. Thus he fulfills the call "to love and care for one's neighbor." As faithful stewards we achieve the primary purpose of business: to serve the user by providing products and services which improve the quality of life and culture.

At Herman Miller we have been blessed with extraordinary people and unusual talent. And because these human resources have created the products and programs which enable us to be at the leading edge, they demand and deserve extraordinary stewardship. The greater the gift, the larger the stewardship obligation. But no matter the size of the gift, in Anne Morrow Lindbergh's words, "One must make a contribution to the world." She is saying, I think, that the faithful stewardship of talents and resources will change the world a little.

Equity, the third principle: Equity involves everyone in the organization. Equity is built on a mutual promise that everyone is granted the opportunity to have equal rights. These include the right to be needed, the right to be involved, the right to be informed and thus to understand, and the right to share in the rewards merited by performance.

A leader must be committed to equity and justice. But first a leader must have integrity, a natural trait that cannot be learned. Nor is integrity enough. For as Samuel Johnson wrote, "Integrity without knowledge is weak and useless, and knowledge without integrity is dangerous and dreadful."

Equity includes justice. Together, they mandate the responsibility of each person to deal fairly and equally with all others, with freedom from bias. Each person must have the opportunity to own the business through personal value added: through suggestions, influences, contributions and performance; and also, at an understood time, each must have an opportunity to be a shareholder owner. These ownerships must be risk ownerships, shared within the business itself and based on the owners' commitment of their lives and resources.

At Herman Miller, we believe the Scanlon Plan provides us with the best tool to manage the business with equity and justice.

Innovation, the fourth principle: Problem solving through innovation must result in products and services which improve the quality of life in the working and healing environments.

But innovation demands risk, and the terms of risk require a willingness and ability to commit to the ideas and influences of people who are able to make unusual connections, to see in new ways, to think at a different level than most of us. These are the innovators. These are the ones who pursue that true innovation which comes from thought and research, not from improvements in engineering.

For true innovation to flourish, leaders must be open to

risk and always ready to accept responsibility for it. We know at Herman Miller that innovation is born of an attitude, a characteristic which flows throughout the organization. It is the result of openness, of a sense of stewardship, and the conviction that owning the business is everyone's business.

Many of us do not know who we are. We drift with the tides and currents created for us by people we label "leaders." Our waking thought each day is, "What can I do today to satisfy me? To be entertained and amused?" We easily convince ourselves, because the situations and events that control our lives are so complex and the problems so vast, that we can do nothing. We think we cannot make a difference.

Collectively, we are a nation adrift. We move from New York to Connecticut to save on taxes, from Minnesota to Florida because it is warmer, from Missoula to Dallas because we are transferred, from a house to a condo and maybe back again—who knows why? Over forty percent of us move at least once every five years.

Businesses are no different. Like individuals, their values are geared to the short haul. They give little thought to the right questions. Such as: Who are we? What are we good at? What should we be doing for society? What difference can we make? Sad to say, these questions are seldom asked.

Business today is beset by the takeover mania. Increasingly, it appears that business is no longer concerned with creating useful products or satisfying service needs. Now, business seems to be the business of buying other businesses. Many managements, it is true, tend to coast, thinking only of themselves and thereby contributing to their own vulnerability. Witnessing such vulnerability does tend to keep one's own management alert to the market and to the best interests of its true owners—the shareholders.

But a company is a social unit, with a history and a culture that have evolved from the goals and actions of many people. A company acquires a style over time that is usually shaped by what's good for everyone whom this social unit comprises, as well as for the shareholders (or employee-shareholders in Herman Miller's case) who own stock because they subscribe to the principles of the company. Almost never, however, do time-honored principles matter to someone taking over a company. New ownership by one man—usually financed by people who don't care, often with junk financing—destroys the employee-owner relationship through which the organization *as social unit* has been built.

But there is a different way of doing business. It is a way that has worked and continues to work today. It is a way that assures people they can influence directions and events; that they can have ownership because of their contribution; that they can work together as a community because they understand and accept the principles that formed the business.

CONNECTION

The difference a business can make, and how it makes it, cannot be divorced from history. History gives us a usable past. And while it may be true, as Emerson writes in his essay titled "History," that "no anchor, no cable, no fence is available to keep a fact a fact," history is nevertheless a starting point for self-examination. Self-examination leads to thinking, and thinking may lead to a clear understanding and acceptance of who we are and where we are going. And knowing where we are going may lead to the mandate for getting there.

Most of the connections in this book are to one company. Reasonably, then, we should begin with the history of that company.

H

erman Miller, like many other companies, begins its story in the early 1900s with a family business. Like a family, Herman Miller was formed by the experiences and lives of those who went before and built its heritage. This heritage began in 1847, when the first settlers, seeking religious freedom and independence, came to Zeeland and Holland, Michigan. The Zeeland group came as an organized church (the only such church other than the Pilgrims, it's widely believed, to arrive in this country as an entity).

The first white man the settlers contacted in the area was a missionary to the Indians. His name—curiously, to those close to Herman Miller—was George Nelson. The first winter for this colony was a bad one. Almost half the people died from cold, lack of food and diseases. But those who survived were stubborn. They had courage, discipline, initiative; and they were resolved to stay and build a community. They did.

In 1905 a group of Zeeland citizens had a defunct canning company on their hands. Acting in accordance with their heritage, they decided that the practical thing to do would be to make furniture in their building.

The new venture's board of directors consisted of familiar Dutch names: Cornelius Roosenraade, William Ossewaarde, Jacob Elenbaas, Martin Elzinga, Isaac Ver Lee, Harry Boone, Johannes Pyle, and John Schipper. They named their business the Star Furniture Company. D.J. De Pree was hired in 1909, fresh out of high school, to perform general office duties.

In 1923, Jacob Elenbaas, the majority stockholder and general manager, became intrigued with oil exploration in Texas. He sold his majority holdings to a group headed by Herman Miller, D.J. De Pree (who had married Herman Miller's daughter Nellie in 1914) and C.J. DenHerder. D.J. shared his recollection of this signal event in interviews with Ralph Caplan for his book, *The Design of Herman Miller*. Caplan writes, "The majority of Michigan Star stockholders were, in De Pree's view, 'neglectful,' and in 1923 Herman Miller, together with D.J. (using borrowed money) bought fifty-one percent of the stock. D.J. called on Jake Elenbaas, the principal stockholder, found him in his vegetable garden, and persuaded him to sell the rest of the stock to associates of Miller. Because he thought 'Michigan Star' was corny, D.J. renamed the company after Herman Miller."

A second, possibly more compelling, reason for the name change was that the company, struggling for survival, might improve its prospects by identifying itself with Mr. Miller, who had become known in the industry as a man of integrity and a manufacturer of quality furniture.

Vital to the history of the Herman Miller Furniture Company was the nature of the early furniture industry. The industry's major centers were Rockford, Illinois; Jamestown, New York; Chicago; New York City; and Grand Rapids. The Grand Rapids manufacturers were the acknowledged leaders, and their conviction that they were the best bordered on arrogance.

Their work was notable, in truth, for its lack of originality. They employed designers whose ideas of furniture were copied from books. Big-time salesmen, working mostly on commission, were allowed by an acquiescent industry to exert a strong influence over the "lines" that got manufactured. They were the ear-to-the-ground department trying to divine what fashions in furniture were going to be *in*. Neither they nor the manufacturers were concerned with the way people lived, only with what would sell.

All of the great Grand Rapids firms were family businesses. Like many family businesses elsewhere, they had a way of deteriorating. Many did fail. Others settled into a comfortable niche in which the owners, if few others, could prosper.

The Herman Miller Furniture Company was no different from its competitors in its fight to survive under discouraging conditions. D.J. De Pree, who became general manager in 1923, has described the early furniture industry's inherent weaknesses in these words:

"The product was sold by commission salesmen who each handled several lines. These lines were displayed in exhibition buildings at several furniture markets. The buyers from the important stores visited these markets, took a look at each line and told the salesmen what pleased them, or displeased them (mostly the latter), about the prices, the designs and quality. Soon, the market situation had deteriorated to the point where they were held four times a year. The demand was always for something new. There was constant guessing by the leading buyers as to whether the popular thing the next season would be Louis XVI, or Queen Anne, or Hepplewhite, or Sheraton, or Adam. This was followed by a scramble on the part of most manufacturers to follow the leaders. The buyers continued to act as the connoisseurs of what was correct, and they were always demanding from the salesmen certain changes in the trim, or the ornamentation or the finish and, most often, the price. Sometimes the changes were as minor as 'putting new buttons on the vest in order to get a different suit.'

"This virtually reduced the manufacturers to mere fabricators with very little control of what they wanted to make and no control of the sale of their product to the people who were going to be long-time users of it. These quarterly changes of designs resulted in a short life for each design, many closeouts sold at damaging discounts and constant sample making for new lines.

"The situation could hardly have been worse, but major changes in the industry added to the serious plight of the small furniture manufacturer.

"Modern furniture plants were established in the southern part of the United States, nearer to the source of much of the lumber being used and where the labor rates were considerably lower. This southern competition, aided by the trading down policies of the stores, became a serious threat to the long-standing leadership of Grand Rapids furniture.''

Desperate as the situation seemed, it suddenly got worse. Events forced the first crisis that was to change the company radically. The stock market crashed in 1929, the Great Depression set in, and Herman Miller faced disaster. Provoked by this crisis, D.J. turned to self-examination, as well as to an examination of Herman Miller and the industry. Here is how he recalls his dilemma:

''I figured we had one year to go before bankruptcy. When you face something like this, you realize something happens inside you. My soul searched and I realized the evils of the industry, which needed correction if I was to stay in business. I listed the following problems in the furniture industry:

Four markets a year.

Short-lived designs and the buyer's first question: What's new?

Closeouts had to be sold, at up to fifty percent off.

Buyer influence, coupled with insufficient knowledge on the part of the buyers.

Commission salesmen. Some had seven to eight lines and sold what was easiest to sell. They showed only what they thought were the very best values, traveled only when they wanted to travel.

Stores took over. We were only a fabricator, with no business identity or plans.

We had no opportunity for repetitive manufacturing.

There was no contact with the ultimate user of the product.

THE BEGINNING

Low wages. Ignoring the ideas of people. Tough attitude toward labor. Responding tough attitude toward management.

Up and down schedules as a result of all this, with layoffs on short notice, uncertain hours, short hours and short paychecks.''

D.J.'s rigorous examination of himself and the business provided a clear understanding of the problem. But where was the solution? It was not long in coming, and its arrival, D.J. believed, was providential. Many years later he described this turning point as if it had occurred the day before:

''On a hot day in July, 1930, a man came into the Grand Rapids showroom and introduced himself as Gilbert Rohde. He talked about his design philosophy. When he talked about his price, $1,000 for the design of a bedroom suite, I thought it was terrible. He had an alternate suggestion, which was three percent royalty to be paid after the furniture was sold. I figured this was a sound arrangement. How could we lose on that?

''Some weeks later, we received our first drawings from Gilbert Rohde. I thought they looked as if they had been done in a manual training school and told him so. 'Eye value' had become very important in selling. He replied with a letter explaining why he designed the way he did. For his designs, there should be utter simplicity: no surface enrichment, no carvings, no moldings. This brought the necessity of precision. We would not cover up with moldings and carvings. He wrote about using the best material for the job; he used chrome tubing where it was structurally better for the purpose. Nothing should cry for attention: 'See what a nice girl I am!'''

In the Grand Rapids world of furniture making, Gilbert Rohde's design theories would have horrified traditionalists. D.J., however, saw merit in them. But his own recollections make it clear that he felt Rohde's social theories about furniture were, if anything, even more significant:

"Gilbert Rohde wrote that furniture should be anonymous. People are important, not furniture. Furniture should be useful. The room is primary. It must be planned for the people who are to live there. He was thinking about people. As a result, the furniture was space saving, utilitarian, multipurpose.''

It was clearly the beginning of a new direction for the Herman Miller Furniture Company. Gilbert Rohde elevated our thinking from selling merely furniture to selling a way of life.

Rohde also began to establish the concept of a broader role for the designer in company affairs. As his letter of January 26, 1935, to D.J. indicates, he moved confidently and firmly into areas of management:

"I do not think you would be making any mistake at all by concentrating more on modern, even if you mean by that dropping everything else.

"I still believe that the living room group you now have is the best for you. There is one thing I hope you will not do, and that is relax any efforts you put behind it. If these efforts are not continued it can easily peter out. Don't let us forget that during the long period of time spent in getting the right sales push behind it, we were handicapped by an entirely inadequate sales force. There is entirely too much evidence that more people are spending money buying goods within that price range, so whatever you do don't get the notion that this is too high priced.''

It is notable that Rohde's emerging intrusion into management prepared the way for George Nelson's much deeper involvement in the years ahead. In 1936 a major decision was made to discontinue period furniture and manufacture only modern furniture of high quality. The reasons for this decision were quite plain. D.J. felt there was a kind of dishonesty in copying old pieces and faking finishes to get an Old World antique look. The country was at the threshold of an era of new materials, tools and techniques.

While problems were being defined and D.J. was making the decisions that would so change Herman Miller, I was in a unique and wonderful position. Change was occurring, ideas were emerging, exciting talent was coming into the business. And I was learning. In later years I would speak to management people about the importance of distinguishing between awareness and involvement. Back then, my position was one of being aware of developments but not truly involved, for my experience was not yet up to the scale of the problems being confronted.

I had graduated from Hope College in 1938 and in June, after the summer furniture market, rode with Jim Eppinger to New York City to begin working half time for him and half for Gilbert Rohde. The pay was terrible, six dollars a week from each of my bosses. But what I learned may have been priceless. I was a gofer, running their errands and doing the little things around the office that no one else wanted to handle. But I was learning about design from Rohde and Irving Harper and Ernest Farmer and about sales from Jim and Gene Eppinger. Living in New York provided the broader outlook I needed in the years to come. The contacts and connections I made then have served me in all the years since.

Jim Eppinger encouraged me to use the understanding and knowledge I was acquiring to return to Zeeland and support D.J. in the wide changes that had to be made throughout the company. I went home in the fall and continued to learn about design and business—the one through reading and studying, and the other through the opportunity D.J. gave me to be aware of the problems and solutions (but with only slowly growing responsibility for them).

From our experience in making both traditional and modern furniture in the same factory, we had learned that in modern we were delivering more furniture per dollar.

BUSINESS AS UNUSUAL

We were also sure that good modern design would have longer life, therefore becoming an answer to every manufacturer's dream for repetitive cuttings of the same components.

This decision had to be made in a marketing climate of apathetic stores and a lack of vision among most of our contemporaries in the industry. We had to pursue our convictions quite single-handedly. We had to go straight to the people who were ready to live with modern design. To reach them, we opened a showroom in New York City, in 1941. Gene Eppinger, manager of that showroom and later the national sales manager, conveys the spirit of the times:

"Did architects and decorators really understand Gilbert Rohde's designs and know how to use them? No, we soon found out, only a few. Who then were the potential customers? They found us, because they wanted to solve their problems of living in a fast-changing Twentieth Century.

"It was immediately apparent that they were not super-rich or high society or overeducated. Rather they were people who were willing to try new ideas, to use unusual shapes and forms and, most of all, to put some order into their daily lives. The Herman Miller showroom person became the space planner, father confessor ('Do you sleep in one or two beds?'), and a guide to a new mode of organizing the home lifestyle.

"Who were these people, and how did they learn? What did they do? That alone would take more time than I have, but I can say that Gilbert Rohde, Elizabeth Kalper, and Ernest Farmer were our faculty. D.J. De Pree and J.M. Eppinger set the rules. I was the ringleader of the first showroom crew. My background was sixteen years of working, improvising, selling, learning and, most important, six months spent in the Rohde office. That was a fantastic experience, where I learned something about furniture design, space planning, the use of color from Irving Harper, and a great deal from Rohde about his philosophy of living in the modern world.

"Can you imagine over six thousand square feet of fantasy, filled with what was then called modern furniture, in 1941? It was a setting so stunning that the visitor could not even imagine living in such an atmosphere. That was the general first reaction. The second thought was, 'Wow! Can I have this? Can I live in this kind of space? What does it take? How much is it and when can I have it?'

"It was fun. We worked six days a week under hot lights and no air conditioning; no real method of managing memos, orders and correspondence. But we did it.

"We talked about 'your furniture,' 'your apartment.' We didn't sell you a seven-piece bedroom and then ask you to try to find room for it. We asked, 'Where are the windows and doors?' 'What is the traffic pattern?' 'Where do you read?' And, again, 'Do you sleep alone?'

"Then came the war and regulations and cutbacks. Herman Miller did its first space planning job. The client was the U.S. Coast Guard Academy in New London; the designer, the Rohde office; and a very shaky, more-nerve-than-brains salesman, Gene Eppinger. The result was an order with AA1 priority for the much needed lumber, etc. What a day!

"Much has been written about the search for a new designer and the providential finding of George Nelson, but we in New York were also learning that more people were ready to accept our direction to a new way of living and organizing their spaces. The demand was there, and now we knew how to reach out and take advantage of our market.

"D.J. agreed that other professional disciplines were needed: public relations, photography, printing, writing. J.M. Eppinger set the pace on selecting our new staff. No one with previous selling experience was really considered. We needed people with imagination and training in the arts and architecture. But most of all we needed people with the desire to spread the word that we can solve your problems of living in the new world: the world of order and smaller spaces, of change and the acceptance of new materials and ideas. Sound familiar? Nothing has changed. But we started it.''

For many of us, the opening of Herman Miller's 1941 showroom in New York was indeed the dramatic turning point Gene Eppinger recalls. But what I remember even more vividly than the opening itself was *getting there*. I had just turned twenty-five and was about to be promoted to the purchasing agent's job. I was also the boss's son, who was sometimes asked to do things nobody else wanted to do—such as making sure that all the furniture to be displayed actually made the truck to New York. I think this may have been my first major task at Herman Miller. And with it came the opportunity to accompany D.J. to the showroom opening.

The morning we were to leave, we discovered a missing piece—a daybed—and I learned an early lesson in crisis management. Jim Eppinger, Gene's uncle and the national sales manager, insisted that this daybed had to be in New York. D.J. promised him that we would take it with us. That afternoon we carried the piece on a car to Kalamazoo, where we were to catch the Wolverine.

D.J. and I each had a lower berth, and he convinced the conductor that there was room for the daybed in our car. Arriving at Grand Central Station, we saw Jim Eppinger waiting on the platform with a porter and a four-wheel handcart. We somehow stowed the daybed on a taxi and completed our expedition to the showroom. It opened on time—and complete.

At Herman Miller a crisis had been faced. A different business was born. The ''evils of the industry'' were being circumvented. The opportunity for a more appropriate quality of life in the home was being offered. The principles by which Herman Miller would pursue its future—the principles of stewardship, equity, trust, risk and innovation—were becoming clear.

But we had not yet arrived. Greater changes were still to come.

BUSINESS AS UNUSUAL

Hy Bomberg
Senior Marketing Manager

Bought a houseful of Herman Miller furniture in 1947; joined the company three years later; was regional sales manager in the early sixties; strong advocate for Propst and Action Office, with a wonderful feeling for Herman Miller and its products.

This is my thirty-sixth year with Herman Miller. Actually, I've been involved for thirty-nine years, because my wife and I, when we decided to get married, happened to go up to the Herman Miller showroom at One Park Avenue in New York, and we fell in love with what we saw there. That was 1947. George Nelson had just introduced the line. We fell in love with what we saw and bought a whole houseful of it. It has survived many moves and three children, and we still own every stick of it today. We had to wait about twenty-six weeks for delivery, so we lived in an apartment with a box spring and a mattress until the furniture arrived. And when it came it was absolutely gorgeous.

At that time, I worked as a furniture salesman in a department store. They had things like "dust proofing." Dust proofing was supposed to be an interesting gimmick that had to do with quality. In fact, as I learned later at Herman Miller, it was just a little piece of plywood to help hold the cabinet together. If a cabinet was made, as it was at Herman Miller — with hand-fitted drawers, with each person who worked on the drawer actually signing it, and it was fitted with runners — then no dust would get in.

Quality meant that you bought things to last. The whole essence of Herman Miller has been the consistency of quality: the ability to design something that would last, not only physically but spiritually, because we're not in the cosmetic design business.

Gilbert Rohde foresaw change. With few exceptions, his work was transitional, carrying Herman Miller from traditional to modern design. The exceptions, such as sectional sofas and cabinets, were ideas ahead of their time.

In 1944 Gilbert Rohde died. A turn had been completed by Herman Miller, and Rohde had played a vital part in it. The direction had been set and no change of course needed to be considered. World War II was on, and since no new products could be introduced, there was time to make a thorough search for a new designer—for someone to continue what Rohde and D.J. had started.

It was natural to look to well-known designers who had demonstrated a kind of thinking similar to Rohde's. Russel Wright, Edward Wormley and others were considered. We even reached a tentative agreement with one of them. But a contrary pattern had already been established at Herman Miller.

D.J.'s search began before war's end, and I was fortunate to have sat in on some of the interviews with candidates while on leave from the Army. In the light of D.J.'s ultimate choice of a successor to Rohde, I recall vividly how hard each of a succession of "name" designers tried to convince us that he alone was uniquely qualified to create our products.

Their absolute certainty notwithstanding, D.J. relied instead on his study
of the industry's failings and the shift to
modern design. He and his close associate Jim Eppinger had been taught that
the predictable way, the "right" way,
was not necessarily the way they should
go.

The designer problem was solved by
doing the "wrong" thing. The successor
to Rohde was a man who had never
designed furniture. He was George
Nelson, an architect, editor, a student of
living, and a perceptive writer about the
furniture industry. His influence on Herman Miller was to be enormous.

In one year, 1946—George Nelson's
first as design director—we introduced
a new kind of furniture for the home.
These designs altered the concepts of
how people should live. Their importance was quick to be recognized by the
national press. In the May 29, 1947, issue
of *Twice A Month,* a mimeographed in-
house newsletter written by D.J. himself,
it was reported that no fewer than eight
architecture and women's magazines
were featuring "the new Nelson line" in
their pages. Of the designer himself, D.J.
wrote, "In spite of George's ability as an
architect, writer and designer, he is very
modest."

Perhaps never has a designer so
changed the philosophy, attitudes, and
direction of a company. George invented
a new role for the designer. He became
involved in the whole business. He be-

came a part of the management of Herman Miller. For good measure, he brought in Charles Eames, Alexander Girard, Isamu Noguchi and other gifted designers. And in a very short time, he designed a "design driven" organization.

Gilbert Rohde's death had led toward another turn, a turn made because Herman Miller's principles as a business had become clear enough to risk letting George Nelson direct the turn. A difference between our company and the rest of the industry was emerging. To a great many people, Herman Miller was heading once again the wrong way down the industry's one-way street.

DESIGN

Lf there is one thing that distinguishes Herman Miller from most other companies, it is our faith in the efficacy of design. Can there be another American corporation, for example, that has strived with such continuity to help all employees of all levels to understand that the organization's fortunes will rise as high as design will take it? Design has truly made the difference at Herman Miller, not only in what we do but in the way we think about what we do.

No one seems to be immune. Joe Schwartz recalled as a senior vice president nearing retirement after thirty-one years with the company, "When I joined Herman Miller, it was a really new experience. What happened is that when I started to look at this product and learn about the designers, I thought, my God, this is really high-quality stuff."

Bill Wiersma, a toolmaker and one of the company's 1978 Frost Award winners, says, "The first day, I couldn't believe my eyes when I walked into the factory. I couldn't believe it! The floors and the colors. The roof was like a rainbow. There was a yellow stripe, then a red stripe, and then a blue stripe. It was just gorgeous. And when it came time to use the bathroom facilities—this is probably going to sound a little humorous—I said to myself, 'This is where I'm going to take my break, right in here. This is the cleanest place. I'm going to have my lunch here!' I hadn't seen the lunchroom then, but I mean it sparkled!"

Nor is Craig Schrotenboer immune. Craig is a manager whose father, Stan, "has worked here more years than I am old." He says, "One of the things that I was always impressed by, growing up and listening to my dad talk and having an opportunity to meet the Eameses, is that they were just driven by a desire to provide honest solutions. We still have a few of the classics in seating, and I hope we always will, because that's a statement in itself of our legacy and our design heritage. That sounds really wild, but I like it. I think it's exciting to be able to say that, to get excited personally about an organization. I have to be able to believe in the products the company sells. My motivation is that they should serve a useful purpose, not just an entrepreneur's need for financial wealth.''

It is quite remarkable that so many in a manufacturing company should make such a subjective value as design so vitally important. We are committed to design, even though it is an elusive process to define.

Today Webster defines design as ''a plan, or scheme conceived in the mind, of something to be done, a preliminary conception of an idea that is to be carried into effect by action.'' A quite inadequate definition.

George Nelson has come closer. He defined design this way: ''Design is an activity that expresses the style, the living rhythm of a society. If any designers think you are or are going to be totally free creative agents, forget it; and if it should happen to you, which heaven forbid, you would have no idea of what to create. Social values provide the framework within which the designer does his job.''

The Gothic cathedrals were designed and built as islands in the midst of poverty, pestilence, and wars. The music played in them was sombre, slow, soul stirring—appropriate because such music created no problems of echo or reverberation. The stained-glass windows were not really windows; they told stories of the Bible to a people who could not read and thus were sources of renewal. These cathedrals provided a marvelous feeling of refuge, joy, peace, and serenity. They were designed and built to solve a problem. They were needed for their time.

Yet the Gothic cathedral's master builder did not think of himself as a designer.

In the medieval castles of England and Scotland, the central problem was safety. A lord's land had been acquired either as a gift from the king or as spoils from battle. Then it had to be protected. No thought was given to protecting an idea or a principle, but only the property and a way of life: that of the owner and occupants. Castles were built on rocks, often surrounded by moats with a drawbridge. Their walls were six or more feet thick, with slots for shooting to repel attackers. Water wells were always inside the castle walls, and a central feature was the keep, or tower, into which the defenders could retreat in a battle.

Yet, eminently suitable to their purpose as castles may have been, they were not the product of a design profession.

In Scotland, during the summers of 1983 and 1984, we lived in a small cottage in Dirleton, a delightful village with castle ruins across the village green. There were no stores, no petrol stations, no main route through town. Dirleton had been laid out hundreds of years ago, simply as a place to live.

Nearby is North Berwick, a larger town with a High Street. North Berwick was obviously not designed for the automobile but for people on foot. The street is narrow, lined with small shops. We walked from one shop to another to buy the goods needed for the next day or two. High Street is now a one-way street for auto traffic. It barely works, and the local people still seem to resent the automobile's intrusion and their need to accommodate it.

Design? The builders of cathedrals and castles had never heard about it. Dirleton and North Berwick were not designed by a designer. But they did reflect, in George Nelson's phrase, the living rhythm of society. The social values and needs of the community did indeed provide a framework for the solutions.

Design as a consciously pursued profession evolved later, when life became more complicated and a need arose for people who could study the problems of living and solve them. Design derives from an understanding of a given problem's inherent nature; and the keener the understanding, the more satisfactory the solution. In the end, design is a professional activity that gives meaningful shape to things.

Yes, but what does such professional activity consist of? What does it take for a person to be able to give meaningful shape to things? I can think of at least three essentials: *creativity, innovation, and hard work.*

Creativity in modern times has been debased as a measure of human achievement. The person in an ad agency who cooks up a new breakfast food "campaign" is called a "creative director." The architect who specifies a Palladian window for a gable wall may be praised for his "creativity." Even football coaches are rewarded for their "creative" formations.

True creativity is something quite different. At its zenith, creativity can be as Tchaikovsky described it occurring while he composed: "Words are vain to tell you the boundless joy that comes over me when a new idea is conceived and begins to take definite shape. One forgets everything. One is a madman trembling and quivering in every organ with scarcely time to outline the sketches, so rapidly does one idea pursue another."

But such moments, Tchaikovsky confessed, are exceedingly fragile: "Sometimes, in the midst of the magic process, an outside shock wakes one from this state of somnambulism. The bell rings, the servant enters, the clock strikes, reminding one that the business of the day must be attended to."

At such moments when inspiration fled, Tchaikovsky fell back on craftsmanship and self-discipline to carry him along. He relied on what he called "a quite cold, deliberate, technical process of work." He felt he had no choice, for as he explained, "An honest artist cannot sit with his hands crossed because he is not inclined to compose. If one waits for inclination, instead of advancing to meet it, one easily drifts into laziness and apathy." Creativity for Tchaikovsky at times also meant hard work.

Fortunately, design does not demand the creative genius of Tchaikovsky. But design is a creative act, and the essence of the creative act is to see the familiar as strange: to look beyond the obvious. The wind had been blowing dust for millions of years, but it was not until 1901 that a man named H.C. Booth thought of using it in reverse. Booth invented the vacuum cleaner.

We may take heart in knowing that a part of the genius of Albert Einstein was his inability to understand the obvious.

Consider plywood. For a product of modern technology, it has a quite long history as a seating material. Gerrit Rietveld designed a chair in 1917 made of flat plywood. Alvar Aalto began using bent plywood in 1930 for his chairs. But it was not until Charles Eames combined his enormous creativity with new ideas and technology that the ultimate expression of the product's potential was realized—in, of course, the sculptural three-dimensional plywood chair.

Without creativity, we do not have design.

The truly creative people form the world's most exclusive club. But despite their rare gifts, they need the help of the rest of us. At Herman Miller, we believe the most rewarding way of focusing design talent is through innovation. Our mandate declares that we will innovate wherever possible. Charles Eames believed we were placing too much emphasis on innovation. He felt our primary emphasis should be on quality, excellence, and improving the product. Nevertheless we are convinced it is this commitment to innovation that gave Herman Miller the ''slight edge'' we've had for so many years.

Innovation needs the right environment. It demands a belief that nothing is sacred, that the ''right'' thing is not automatically the way to go. Innovation is a result of a creative act, or a series of creative acts. It is achieved through a willingness to risk. It is achieved through a climate of openness, a readiness for anything. Bruce Burdick said, "If, in designing, you pursue a design idea logically, it is likely that someone else has done it before. The need is to work on the idea and see what accidents happen, and then pursue those."

Innovation, like creativity, is hard work.

George Nelson, in the first Eames Memorial Lecture, said, "Creativity takes a lot of very dirty work." For Charles Eames, the last ten percent of any design was always the most difficult.

On a visit to India, Charles became fascinated with the lota, a vessel that the people of India have used for hundreds of years for carrying liquids, grain, clothing and other provisions. He proposed a series of considerations that he felt would need to be faced in order to create such a product today.

"First," he said, "shut out all preconceived ideas and begin to consider factor after factor: the optimum amount of liquid to be fetched, carried, poured, and stored in a prescribed set of circumstances; the size, strength, and gender of the hands that would manipulate it, the way it is to be transported—head, hip, hand, back—the center of gravity when empty, when full; its balance when rotated for pouring; its sculpture as it fits the palm of the hand, the curve of the hip; the relation of opening to volume in terms of storage uses and objects other than liquid; heat transfer; can it be grasped if the liquid is hot; how pleasant does it feel, eyes closed, eyes opened; how does it sound when it strikes another vessel; what is the possible material; what is the cost in terms of working; what is the cost in terms of ultimate service; how will the material affect the contents?"

To an astonishing degree, the thought process Charles applied in conceiving of a hypothetical product to replicate the lota is the same process he and Eero Saarinen actually used in designing their chair for the Museum of Modern Art competition of 1941. Here is how he responded when asked what is the "trick" to winning competitions:

"This is the trick, I give it to you, you can use it. We looked at the program and divided it into the essential elements, which turned out to be thirty odd. And we proceeded methodically to make one hundred studies of each element. At the end of the hundred studies we tried to get the solution for that element that suited the thing best, and then set that up as a standard below which we would not fall in the final scheme. Then we proceeded to break down all logical combinations of these elements, trying to not erode the quality that we had gained in the best of the hundred single elements; and then we took those elements and began to search for the logical combinations of combinations, and several of such stages before we even began to consider a plan. And at that point, when we felt we'd gone far enough to consider a plan, worked out study after study and on into the other aspects of the detail and the presentation.

"It went on, it was sort of a brutal thing, and at the end of this period, it was a two-stage competition and sure enough we were in the second stage. Now you have to start; what do you do? We reorganized all elements, but this time, with a little bit more experience, chose the elements in a different way, (still had about twenty-six, twenty-eight, or thirty) and proceeded: we made a hundred studies of every element; we took every logical group of elements and studied those together in a way that would not fall below the standard that we had set. And went right on down the procedure. And at the end of that time, before the second competition drawings went in, we really wept, it looked so idiotically simple we thought we'd sort of blown the whole bit. And won the competition. This is the secret and you can apply it."

Yes, of course.

Hard work involves users, salespeople, engineers, craftsmen, manufacturers, researchers. It involves a team. Without the hard work of these and others, creativity and innovation and a good design cannot occur.

So now we have shifted from design to *good* design. Bad design seems much easier to identify than good design. We see it in most suburban housing, in American taxicabs, in a Boeing 737 where the cramped seating seems to be for midgets only. It is easy to ignore creativity and innovation, to design quickly without hard work. Bad design is easy. But what is good design?

Once, in discussing the design of Herman Miller's New York showroom, the words "good design" were used. Charles Eames said, "Don't give us that good design crap. You never hear us talk about that. The real questions are: Does it solve a problem? Is it serviceable? How is it going to look in ten years?"

Charles taught us that design must have an objective; that originality for its own sake can only be disastrous; that if you pursue an objective to its logical conclusion, then you can get something good for your efforts. Such a pursuit is not easy, however, because many unforeseen difficulties and mistakes will be encountered between your recognition of an objective—which in itself is a big accomplishment—and its logical conclusion.

What do we know about design? We know that design is, at a minimum, a plan or a scheme. We know that design is an activity which expresses the living rhythm of a society, and that a designer works within a framework provided by the social values of his time. We also know that design gives a meaningful shape to things; that in the active pursuit of design we have to be alert to the unexpected, to accidents. We know that a good design must have an objective; and, most certainly, design requires creativity, innovation and hard work.

Whenever most of us think about designers, which we seldom do, we bog down in considerations of aesthetics and taste. We think of designers as stylists who make a product attractive so people will buy it. But designers don't, can't, and shouldn't work that way. Then how should they work? What do they do? Who, in short, is a designer?

Designers, like engineers, executives, doctors and lawyers, need to learn the process through which they are engaged and their work is valued. They must understand a responsibility to society, then commit themselves to making a valid contribution. First, however, the designer needs to be designed: The designer needs the training and education to become a prepared professional.

Each of us should know who we are, but for a designer this is most important. Without a deep self-awareness, there will be no effective design. The designer needs to study life around him, to understand people and their needs. George Nelson once said, in answer to a question about how designers work, ''People are more like people than like cows or pigs, so if a designer has studied a need and solved it to his own satisfaction, then there probably are other people who need the same solution.''

A designer without creative ability is a stylist, or a draftsman. But where there is creative ability, it must be paired with understanding, acceptance and commitment to the creative process. Bruce Burdick, in *The Human Resource*, notes that great artists, scientists and thinkers are people who do these things: challenge assumptions, recognize patterns, see in new ways, make connections, take risks, take advantage of chance, and construct networks.

More than anyone else, a designer who uses these resources can bring to an organization a spirit of creativity.

A designer should seek innovation wherever possible but shouldn't confuse it with ''something new.'' This leads to a particularly sad kind of surrender: to original-ity for its own sake. Perhaps this has been one of the prob-lems with Italian furniture design in recent years. The de-signer's objective is originality, rather than the solution to a problem. This may well be because no problem was defined. The designer had no objective. The quality of the solution will depend, not on a reach for originality, but on the completeness of the problem's definition and the objective.

Designing without an objective is like a Sunday after-noon ride through the country. It may be a pleasant ex-perience, but it doesn't get you anywhere. To get some-where, designers must be committed to solving problems, in an innovative way if possible, but in any case only after they have clearly defined the problem and set an objective.

Designers must also be opportunists looking for the ac-cidents that happen along the way. George Nelson was studying interior walls in 1945 as part of his architectural practice when he saw that these walls could be made deeper. Drawers, cabinets and closets could then be incor-porated. The result, his famous Storage Wall, changed the way people viewed interior space and how it could serve them.

Penicillin, the first antibiotic, was discovered by acci-dent when Alexander Fleming found a mold he wasn't looking for growing on a culture of some common germs.

At noon in the tiny harbor at Dunbar, Scotland, all the boats not out at sea fishing, large and small, are lying on their sides in the mud. Only an hour and a half later, large fishing boats are coming toward the harbor through the narrow channel in the high rocks on a swiftly rising tide. Only local knowledge enables the skippers to time their fishing and their homecoming.

Like them, the designer needs to know what's going on. He needs to know the policies, goals, and direction of the organization—but also how and why things work, and who makes them work. And he had better understand the politics in the organization or nothing will be brought to market.

The designer's task is complicated. He must see the organization from the perspective of the chief executive officer, but also through the eye of the foreman, the craftsman and many others in between. He is the force that connects the various skills and talents needed and leads them through the objective.

How this is done depends on the designer. Just as there are different successful styles of management, so there are different styles of design. The designers we have worked with at Herman Miller have used the knowledge and resources available to them in different ways (and we will discuss them in our next section). But each one of them always knew the company intimately because he had the opportunity not only of designing the company's products but also of helping to design the company itself.

Never should a designer be disconnected during the development of a product, a system or a service. He must be a leader, to make sure that the appropriate or relevant skill is brought to bear on the design. Although the nature of that leadership role may change during the development process—just as management's role may change—the designer is always the control connection. If that fails— if one of the other fields dominates and the designer is disconnected—the quality of the solution will suffer.

The designer requires the active involvement of the appropriate talent and people in the organization. In turn, these people expect the designer to be their teacher. But to teach what? The designer can teach the organization how to think. How to see. How to be creative. How to work through a process. How to take advantage of accidents. And how the need for quality and excellence is imperative.

The designer is by compulsion a teacher. I can think of no effective designer who did not also teach. A designer who teaches is enabling those with whom he works to broaden their perspective, to become more aware of the importance of design as a driving force in the organization. And the designer benefits, too. He is building connections which will enable him to make an ever-growing contribution.

So we can say that the right designer will produce appropriate solutions to an organization's needs when he is allowed to work within the context of that organization, its people, philosophy and goals. If he feels himself a part of the organization, he will be more effectively involved in setting specific objectives. This does not mean, however, that "inside" designers will perform better. To the contrary, insiders tend to become inbred and bogged down by too great an intimacy—by too many connections, too much company politics. As a result, the need for solving problems most likely will be tailored to fit the style of the person to whom they report.

Few designers can do their best work in a setting of competitions or design workshops, such as Philip Rosenthal's in the 1950s and 1960s. Rosenthal's worked only because the timing was right and the products were appropriate. Today, I see such competitions as unworkable, made obsolete by the need for a design-led team to tackle the increasingly complicated problems posed by new technology, as well as the need for speed in development. Anyway, seldom have we seen a lasting design come by that route. The Museum of Modern Art once sponsored such competitions. In one, the prize-winning chair never made it to market because it could not be produced. An also-ran in that same competition, the Eames plastic chair, is still in production, still useful, still appreciated. And why? Because the designer knew and was involved in the technology and manufacturing process.

The designer makes a difference.

THE DESIGNERS

Joseph Schwartz
Senior Vice President, retired

Joined Herman Miller as a salesman; led the introduction of Action Office with innovative marketing and sales programs; as senior vice president, was responsible, first, for design and research, then moved to marketing and sales; phenomenal ability to immerse himself in a new program and bring it to the market.

You have got to be a mental giant in order to master Herman Miller's management. Stumpf is a mental giant. Whether Bill is right or wrong, whether any of them are right or wrong, their communication skills, their ability to articulate a vision, and their ability to paint a picture is what it takes. That is what it takes, with passion, to get Max or me or anybody else at Herman Miller to say, "I want to follow this guy." You see, we are always looking for a giant. We have this messianic thing built into the company. We need a giant for a designer, a guy who is no dummy, who doesn't sit there with nothing to say, who can paint the big pictures that say to Herman Miller, "We are going to elevate where we are to this level, take the next step in our development, and I am going to help you get there."

We don't know how to get there by ourselves and we need this person. Some of the things that we have done that haven't worked, that were designed internally which never cut the mustard, have taught us that we don't know how to get there ourselves. Which is why we have changed and created more outside design resources.

I once said to Stumpf, "We are selling all these workstations and we are losing all the chairs. We don't have a darned chair to sell with an AO station. We will sell a guy 1,000 workstations and he'll buy 3,000 chairs from Steelcase or from Knoll or somebody else. Of course," I said, "the plastic chairs are too small, too hard. The soft pads are not appropriate, and they are too expensive." I said, "We need some office chairs." And that is how the Ergon chair was born.

Bill Stumpf was available. He didn't know anything about designing furniture; he'd never designed any furniture in his life. But we staked him. The reason Hugh staked him, I'm sure, was because Bill had the mind. He had the verve. You can see, as in a mirror, the way Nelson and Eames and Propst used to think and the way Stumpf approaches a problem.

That has been the driving thing that has given us design con-
fidence. Not the fact that these guys designed everything before
we hired them, but because they had the ability to think about
a problem.

Robert Propst
Former President, Herman Miller Research Corporation

Conceived and brought to life Action Office, Coherent Structures for the hospital, Action Factory, and much, much more;
radically changed not only Herman Miller's direction, but also
life and work in innumerable places.

Our aspiration has always been to design things that are
fashion-proof: that have more quiet, enduring qualities; that try
to retreat to more elementary qualities. To me, the real nature
of good design is found in things that have long-term attributes;
that you can really live with a long time; that you don't get jaded
with or tired of—so that your life will be filled with other more
interesting values than trying to disturb this manneristic place
where you live.

We've never had a project where we didn't want the best in
design skill. But if you've wrapped yourself in a design image,
you're going to be a very uninfluential person in matters that
count. The way to look at it is that designers are almost the last
people who have access to problems. They very seldom have a
strong voice in any interesting decisions or commitments. They
are mainly involved in the world of trying to clean up and make
things attractive, so that in most cases they have an incredibly
mundane perception of what things should be.

We say that whatever forces we may carry, we've got to escape
from this horribly debilitated posture that designers find them-
selves in. We've got to have access to problems on a first-rate
basis. We've got to have access to terrific authority. We've got
to be able to deal with people at first-rate levels. We'll never get
through any of those doors by saying, "We've got design!"

I t was providential that Gilbert Rohde's ideas and designs solved the problems, as D.J. defined them, of both Herman Miller and the "evils" of the furniture industry. This combination provided the first major turning point in the life of Herman Miller.

Rohde had the ability to teach, and D.J. had the willingness to learn. Rohde's continuing thesis was quite simple: Forget about public taste and trends. Forget about producing what you think will sell in the next furniture market. Concern yourselves instead with researching and answering certain human needs in the home environment.

An apt student, D.J. said later, "He taught us new responsibilities and disciplines for the manufacturer. First, the designer was to retain absolute control over the production of his creations. The manufacturer would not be allowed to change the mechanics or appearance of a design to the slightest degree.

"Second, the materials used in the production of a design were to be respected for their inherent qualities. The manufacturer would not be allowed to use a material in a manner unnatural to its basic character. There was to be, for example, no faking of finishes.

"Third, the manufacturer was not to produce copies of antiques but rather devote his energies to producing furniture *of the day*, embodying the best available contemporary materials to solve problems of living and working in the home."

And so Herman Miller, in the early 1930s, became the first company in the U.S. to mass-produce a broad range of modern furniture, offering a change in the way people could live.

After Gilbert Rohde's death, during the war, D.J. selected George Nelson to be Herman Miller's designer. A number of compelling reasons dictated his choice. George's work as an editor and writer at *Architectural*

Forum had caught his eye, and though still a young architect, George had already gained recognition as a Rome Prize winner and promising practitioner. But most of all, I am sure, D.J. was captivated by the breadth of George's mind and the eloquence of his expressed ideas.

Many years later, in an interview with Mildred Friedman, editor of *Design Quarterly,* George recalled how he happened to be hired: "I felt obliged to tell this utterly sincere and good man that I really didn't know much about furniture. D.J. listened very solemnly, and when I told him to go look for a designer who had been in a furniture factory, he said, 'O.K.' And he went.

"I forgot all about them. They were gone for like four to six months, and suddenly they came back. 'It's very nice to see you,' I said, 'but what are you back for?' D.J. said, 'Well, we did see a lot of designers who knew a lot about furniture and everything. You have no idea how many telegrams we got before poor Gilbert Rohde was cold in his grave, from people who were going to lead us to the Promised Land.' Then D.J. told me they had gone and visited every one of them. He said, 'We talked to them and looked at their stuff. They were all just terrible. All their furniture was awful.'"

Mickey Friedman interrupted George to ask, "How did he know this? Was it instinct?"

George replied, "This was a very honest man. He had a nose for fakery. He understood dishonesty. It wasn't so much aesthetics, but if a thing struck him as not an honest statement of whatever it was supposed to be, all the bells started ringing and the red lights went on. This is what protected him.

"Then D.J. said, 'So we're back because we figured that all these experts being as bad as they are, we couldn't do worse than get somebody who didn't know anything. So how about it?' So we made a deal."

What a deal it was. Within one year, George Nelson and his associates, with the unending cooperation of a few key

Herman Miller people like Bill Staal, brought to the market an exciting line of furniture for all areas of the home. Never since have we duplicated such an effort and program in so short a time.

D.J. and his new designer hit it off from the beginning. In a letter dated October 5, 1945, George expressed both his optimism and his candor: "Our meetings in New York were perfectly swell. I can't tell you what a pleasure it was to see so many decisions made with such speed. I think that from here in, my only problem will be to produce."

George later spoke of this feat in his pithiest manner. "I got hold of Ernest Farmer, who had worked with Rohde, and between us we concocted that first show of seventy-odd pieces. That was about a year and a half's work. Now if they can do six pieces in three years, it's good. But in those days they turned out seventy-odd pieces in a year and a half because they had no facilities, no extra people, no engineers, no researchers, no nothing. It gives you pause."

Those products and designs were the first and most visible part of the second turning point in the life of Herman Miller. But there was much more to come.

George Nelson was one of those rare people who could not only do the job expected of him, but always went far beyond expectations, expanding the job and thereby increasing his contribution to the organization. He saw design as a larger consideration than product design. He saw the need for designing the company.

Very quickly, he began designing advertising, literature and catalogs. He proposed an outrageous idea: "Let's sell our catalog." We did, and nearly four decades later it is a collector's item. In those days, full-page ads in color in trade magazines were unheard of and far beyond our budget (though we really didn't have one). George convinced us that this was necessary, and it was done. His showroom designs were models for industry, stores, architects and designers.

All of this gave us recognition, establishing the image of the company as a leader, one that was making a contribution to life in the home, that was going to be an important factor in the industry. Herman Miller had made another turn, and we were headed in a new direction.

George, however, did not think what had been done was enough. He knew who he was, what he could not do. And he knew others who could do some things better.

As an editor of the *Forum* in 1940, George had known of Charles Eames and Eero Saarinen and the design work they were doing together, and particularly of their exhibit that year at the Museum of Modern Art. The three became acquainted and visited occasionally.

In 1946, Eames invited George to the Berkshire Hotel in midtown Manhattan, where he showed him drawings and parts of some molded plywood chairs. George was surprised, because he had thought of some of these same ideas himself. Here was Charles Eames, who had already done the work.

George phoned D.J., who came with James Eppinger, his longtime associate and friend, to see Eames' work. By then it was on exhibit at the museum. George urged D.J. to sign Eames. Knoll was wooing him, but they had labor problems and Charles did not like the way they were handling them. George told Charles that Herman Miller had no such problems and urged him to join our company.

Then George had second thoughts: "This guy might take my place!" He tried to discourage the whole idea, but later decided that if Eames was going to be a better designer, why not have him at Herman Miller rather than with the competition? So late one night he phoned D.J. and convinced him to go ahead. (Among their other enthusiasms, George and D.J. shared a craving—along with the two Eppingers, Jim and Gene—for hot fudge sundaes at Rumplemyer's in New York. After seeing the Eames chair exhibit at the Museum of Modern Art, they all went to Rumplemyer's and each had two sundaes.)

George brought in Charles Eames, who had designed the molded plywood chairs, and then Alexander Girard, as the need for a textile program became clear. The three of them worked individually and together. They exchanged ideas, supported each other, made connections, both inside and outside Herman Miller. They designed a complete program.

What kind of men were they? How did they work? What did they design? What was it like to work with them?

George Nelson: He Redesigned the Company

Initially, George Nelson was the leader. During their long relationship with each other and Herman Miller, there was no professional jealousy between Nelson and Eames. Personal differences did develop, however, and as the years went by, George and Charles seldom worked together. Meanwhile, Charles and "Sandro" Girard not only worked together but continued to be good friends.

George Nelson's work gave us the foundation for a highly developed, coordinated design program. He provided Herman Miller with a steady flow of new design ideas. It was he who searched out new techniques and materials and combined them with traditional craftsmanship.

George may have been the finest marketing man Herman Miller ever had, because he sensed trends and knew how to respond with solutions. More than any other person, he changed the field of interior design. But he knew that for him personally, as well as for Herman Miller, this was not good enough.

George's talent was broad. His curiosity, thinking and ideas needed wider opportunity. He began to make exciting excursions into other fields. He designed the Chrysler Exhibit and the Irish Pavilion at the New York World's Fair. With Charles Eames and Alexander Girard, he wrote and designed a communications course, using sound, slides, movies, and even smell for the University of Georgia. It bore the daunting title "A Rough Sketch for a

Sample Lesson for a Hypothetical Course.'' In 1959, George designed the U.S. Exhibit in Moscow, a staggering assignment. In nine months he had to design and build a show which communicated the American way of life to a people whose experience preconditioned them to doubt what they saw. Three hundred thousand square feet of space had to be designed. He brought in Charles Eames, who created a seven-screen movie which portrayed the face of America to the Russians.

George designed appliances for General Electric, wrote books and articles on design, and he practiced architecture. His prefabricated and experimental aluminum home showed the advantages possible in the use of technology for residential homes.

Once, when I was driving with George to visit a Charlotte, Michigan, manufacturer, he remarked that most of us use only ten to twenty percent of our capacity. George probably used more of his capacity than any person I have known, but he thought so clearly, so easily, so quickly about so many subjects, that it was difficult for him to bring projects to completion. He seemed to lack discipline, especially during the waning years of our relationship. ''He had all the talents,'' it has been said, ''but the talent to use them.''

Nevertheless, working with him was always a joy and at times breathtaking. Often our agenda would be set aside, and George would express some vision of a solution to our urban blight, or to a political crisis. It was fascinating but frustrating. I once suggested he give up his office and do nothing but write, since that seemed to be the only work he would complete. A long period of silence followed that nearly broke our relationship.

It was providential, fortuitous, plain lucky and the result of hard work that this working friendship between Herman Miller and George Nelson was formed, developed and carried on. At that time, he was so important to Herman Miller that without him the company could well have ceased to exist. There is no doubt that George Nelson was the most creative designer in our lives. He worked closely with engineering, manufacturing, sales and marketing people. He used these and other associates, but sometimes he felt great scorn for what he considered their lack of necessary know-how or commitment.

George was not only a designer at Herman Miller but also a leader, a consultant, a resource, a teacher. He contributed so much but was recognized so inadequately. We who knew him would never be the same.

Charles Eames: Making It As Good As It Can Be

Charles Eames was a different kind of designer. He differed from George Nelson in personality, style and the way he worked. During the late fifties his designs were our major program, and both the quality of his work and the quality of his communication gained him worldwide recognition. The late Eliot Noyes, an architect and industrial designer of renown, said, ''After the first Eames chair development right after World War II, no furniture anywhere in the world was being designed that wasn't influenced by it.''

Great success came to him because he had great personal discipline, was obsessed with quality and excellence, made outrageous demands on those who worked for and with him, had few clients and concentrated on fewer projects. The distinguished M.I.T. scientist, Philip Morrison, who sometimes offered Charles learned advice on his film projects, saw him in a singular light: ''People like to see unity in the world. And there is deep unity in the world. The work of Eames stands as enormous unity of its own.''

Charles could so clearly define the objective. Then he would begin a trial-and-error, recycling process: always refining, redesigning, making hundreds of small changes, sometimes starting over again. Once, during the development of the plastic chair, he could not find the right combination of materials and technology. He switched to an entirely different material and designed the wire chair, which is still being made in Europe today.

His description, in the April, 1958, issue of *Interiors* magazine, of how he and his wife, Ray, worked is worth pondering:

"When Ray and I did the molded plywood chair, we set out deliberately to develop an economical and feasible method for molding plywood. This was the first step in developing a chair which we hoped would have good qualities, but whose qualities we insisted would be inherent in the mass production system and have their basis in the mass production method. . . . The molded plastic chair was much different. The reinforced polyester was a special technique developed for areas that demanded a high performance of material. . . . Our object was to make this high-performance material accessible to the consumer in a chair that would ultimately give it a high performance per dollar. The problem wasn't so much one of form. . . . The real problem was to make this essentially industrial material available at the consumer level.

" . . . the beginnings of the cast aluminum chair were entirely different. This one started when Alexander Girard, Sandro, came to visit and we were talking about furnishing a house which he and Eero (Saarinen) had just completed . . . Sandro was bemoaning the fact that there was no real quality outdoor furniture. . . . You start on a close human scale. Here is a friend who has done something. He needs something for it, and you become involved. As we were trying to analyze the reasons why there was nothing available on the market to suit him, why we were of course starting to write a program for designing the object to fill this void. . . . This was not like the beginnings—or even the motives—of the other chairs. The story of those was mostly of sticking to a concept. . . . This was more like an approach to an architectural problem, where you have the program fairly well embedded and call on past experience."

DESIGN AT HERMAN MILLER

The variety of work Charles did for his clients was as good as he could make it. He had to feel right about it. He put so much of himself into it. He was never easily satisfied. He liked working in the movie industry because it demanded discipline. One day he took us to the set of *Irma La Douce* to teach us that while it was possible to relax between takes, the minute Billy Wilder called "Action" the set was transformed into a place of intensity and professionalism. It was a lesson for each of us about performance.

Charles was, of course, a great filmmaker himself. We and others still use his films. He experimented with multiple screens, leading the way for development by others of this communication form. His largest and best productions were those he did for the Moscow exhibition in 1959, for the science building at the Seattle Century 21 Exposition, and the IBM building at the 1964 New York World's Fair.

His exhibits for IBM on Copernicus and the computer, *Mathematica*, his work for the State Department, his exhibitions in France and India—all were masterpieces of communication.

How was it to work with Charles Eames, as his client? On visits to his office, there was a ritual that had to be observed. First the greeting, usually by Ray. Then an invitation to look at some new ideas, mostly having nothing to do with Herman Miller; or, alternately, a review of a current major project or perhaps a showing of the latest version of a film.

There would follow a beautifully organized lunch, always supervised by Ray. Then a bit of fun, perhaps with Charles playing the organ grinder. By midafternoon we might be given a look at any progress on a design for Herman Miller. Often, little or none was to be seen.

Finally, we would go into the conference room, close the door, and talk. That is when the real work began. I would bring out my agenda. We almost never looked at it after that, but instead would talk about Herman Miller's needs and problems as he saw them. He probed and pushed, always waiting for feedback, making sure that he and Herman Miller were not going off in different directions. Then, suddenly, he might disappear to prod someone else, or to find the answer to a question that had popped up during our conversation. He knew how to make use of an accident.

In the last several years of our friendship, Charles and I seldom talked about design. He was obsessed with quality, with making every product better. He probed: Is the Lounge Chair being made as good as it can be? Who is deciding on changes in materials? Who at Herman Miller cares about quality? How do they show they care? What exactly are you doing, Hugh, about quality? Few answers would satisfy him. One time, he was so persistent that I stood up and said I would leave if he did not ease off. He invited me to go. Only Ray, flittering nervously about, doused the fire we had suddenly and uncharacteristically set. She persuaded us to resume the lunch she had set for us. We did, but he still talked about quality.

So working with Charles Eames was a high for me and many others. One's level of understanding and care was raised beyond expectations. But it was not easy. It was difficult to deal with the contradictions of fun and intensity. It was hard sometimes to understand him. But, oh my, was it ever worth it.

Ralph Caplan once said, ''Charles Eames was not always teaching, but when you were with him you were always learning.''

Alexander Girard: A Gift of Excitement

Sandro Girard had the same drive for quality as Charles Eames, but with even more concern for detail. He had a superb feeling for color and texture, and his ability to fit together bits and pieces into a meaningful whole was inimitable. He was a master of surprise. We never knew what to expect on visits to Sandro and Susan's home in Santa

Fe. It might be a new Indian artifact he had collected, or dinner in a new restaurant he had designed, or a mad ride through the Indian country. One time, with Susan driving, Sandro, Charles and I rode all day from one pueblo to another, stopping often to photograph a flower or a gravestone. Sound like work? No, but it was part of the learning experience that makes Herman Miller what it is today.

With Sandro Girard, when it was work it was all work. But work was fun, too, because he had such a marvelous ability to put colors, patterns and ideas together. If we had planned a review for the textile program, everything would be superbly organized with detailed information, swatches and sales figures displayed on walls and tables. He knew what was right. He was tough and demanding in achieving, through us, what he saw was needed.

We followed Alexander Girard where he led us because we knew he had impeccable taste and incredible astuteness about space, color, and pattern. He provided for the Herman Miller program an emotional enrichment which made a vast difference. For those of us who were fortunate to have worked with him, particularly in Santa Fe, he gave us a sense of joy and pleasure. He taught us that fun in work is an ingredient that carries us past the small crises we face.

For a while, he had a great deal to do with making us well known, maybe even more so than Eames did. He did this through the kinds of places he designed. He designed an exhibit at the Grand Rapids Furniture Museum and some rooms for the Detroit Institute of Art, among his many notable projects. All of his work was striking enough that the architecture and interiors magazines latched onto it, thereby giving Herman Miller a lot of publicity.

Then there was Girard's fabulous San Francisco showroom. How it came about was the result of still another fortuitous encounter. We had made the decision to have a showroom in San Francisco, and D.J. had gone out and decided on a certain building. It had been a warehouse for herbs and spices and smelled just wonderful. But before closing the deal, he asked if I would take a look at it with Girard and Eames.

So the three of us paid this warehouse a visit and agreed with D.J. that it was a pretty nice building. We decided, however, that we would think about it over lunch. As we were looking for a place to eat in the neighborhood, we came across another building. It revealed little of itself to us, because its front was covered with sheets of plywood. Intrigued, we made a few inquiries and learned that the building had once housed a sporting establishment, with a restaurant downstairs and small rooms above where the hostesses and their clients might retire after dinner.

At the urging of both Girard and Eames, I commandeered a hammer and crowbar and went to work stripping off the plywood. Marvelous ornamentation began to appear, and we soon could see that this had been a superb building. Girard got all excited, so we went looking for the owner. He let us inside, and we discovered that the interior details, when uncovered and exposed, were just as wonderful as what we'd seen on the street.

That night, I phoned D.J. and said, ''We've decided we don't like your building. We've found another one we like much more. Would it be okay if we take ours?'' I don't think he had all that much faith in his son's architectural judgment, but he did in Girard's and Eames'. He gave us his approval, following which we managed to call off the tentative arrangement with the owners of the spice warehouse and made a deal for our own great discovery.

Girard's rare gift for excitement, detail and color made the San Francisco showroom a brilliant polychromatic landmark during the 1960s. He applied the same design skills in creating another of Herman Miller's critical successes—the Textiles and Objects Shop in midtown Manhattan. Neither of these exciting environments has survived; our needs in San Francisco outgrew the showroom, and the T & O Shop was a financial failure. Nevertheless they gave Herman Miller great distinction and, among people who remember them today, they still do.

Three giants—George Nelson, Charles Eames, and Alexander Girard—provided designs that were so clearly solutions to needs, so different and so completely thought out, that they quickly dominated the company. From their successes, the need to redesign the entire company emerged.

If the role of the designer was clear, what about management's? The climate of freedom was provided by management. It was management's belief that the designer's decisions were as important as anyone's. Further, since good design could only take place in a climate of freedom, a commitment had to be made to the certainty of production. The role of management—together with engineering, manufacturing, sales and marketing—was to provide feedback.

Sometimes this feedback defined the objective, as it did with the seating for Chicago's O'Hare Airport. Ed Murphy, our Chicago sales manager, had made a working connection with C.F. Murphy Associates (no relation), the architects for the new terminal. We arranged a meeting between Charles Eames and the architects to discuss their objectives for seating. We gave him the freedom to work out the solution, and he designed the seating which is still in use at O'Hare. The feedback from sales ultimately put Herman Miller into the airport seating business. We supplied airport seating the next few years for most of the major terminals in this country and several abroad.

Management began to work with designers, not only on the objectives but the boundaries of the problem. The objectives, we learned, could be seen much more clearly if the constraints were defined. Sometimes, however, we still looked with worshipful stance to the designer for the solution. George Nelson would complain that we were often asking him "to design us out of our problems."

We were closing a period in our history—"designer as God." So much responsibility could no longer be borne perpetually by so few men. Furthermore, another era was taking shape. Problems in living were more complex. New technologies were being invented and new methods developed. We began to see that it would take a highly professional team, including the designer, to command the available information in addressing the needs of today. At Charles Eames' urging, we organized a technical center and staffed it with professional engineers. Charles gave them their objective: "Make our products unassailable in the marketplace." We brought in other talent to support the designer and enable him to solve problems more effectively.

So the role of designer and management changed. In his day, the arbitrariness of Gilbert Rohde was good. But it could not last. The team approach—with appropriate leadership changing as needs of the project changed— works even today; and yet the designer's decisions continue to be important.

It is the responsibility of management to establish, from the feedback and constraints, a framework. Within this framework, objectives are set and the problem defined. The designer is involved in this process. The designer is a problem solver and must be able then to work within a climate of freedom, for this is necessary if he is to make an effective contribution. This climate he earns through his performance and responsible acceptance of the trust that management gives him.

Together we are problem solvers, and problem solving for people's needs occurs through identifying, studying, and investigating with a team; assembling and filtering not only information on needs but also materials and technology. This kind of process leads best to innovation in an organization.

Our relationship at Herman Miller with each of our designers has been fruitful, and stormy. Our designers have often proposed doing the "wrong" thing. Together, we had failures such as the Eames storage units for dormitories. Designers do make mistakes. Management may be arrogant and deaf, thereby degrading a sensitive relationship. For as Jack Kelley, a seasoned observer, says, "Designers always have a tremendously tough time bringing forth things. You're always battling, always at the crux of the issues all the time. Because, well, somebody else might have a better idea, but, for crying out loud, maintain the opportunity to bring design and the solutions to the marketplace."

Tension, crisis and contradiction are facts of life. We did have many difficult times together. But there is a basic reason for Herman Miller's continuing vitality as a living organization today; reason enough for each of us to be part of what has become a worldwide organization. It can be summed up on one word—design, design done by designers who have led, supported and been a part of the business named Herman Miller.

Thomas Pratt
Senior Vice President

Began in sales; responsible for marketing and sales during much of the time of rapid growth; then assumed his present position as responsible for research and design.

It seems that our problem at this company was figuring out how to reproduce the patron-artist relationship that occurred between D.J. and George Nelson. We learned, for instance, that Hugh never quite bonded in the same way with Nelson as D.J. did. But yet there was a new bond formed between Hugh and Bob Propst, and that bond was never reproduced by anybody else. We have never been able to revive it. But we learned something about bonding, and today we have design program managers with good design sensitivity—some of them design-trained themselves—who have been able to facilitate and enable a designer to bond with us in a way that wasn't possible before.

Through his or her personal and professional relationship with the designers, a program manager enables the designer to be very, very, clear about how a project plan is connected with the company vision—with the mandate. We like to say that the product planning strategy or the thought process behind strategic product planning starts with a mandate that embodies much of our vision and gives direction to our efforts. We go from these broad directions given to us by the Herman Miller mandate to a more focused mission statement for each part of the business, and from these statements, specific product and project strategies and criteria evolve.

I think we have found the way to bond with a broader number of designers. Many say it cannot be done; you know, the notion that you can only have one or two big designers at a time. But before long I think we will have demonstrated another way to see things and will have practiced it enough that it will become a part of our culture—part of our way of relating to and working with designers.

Herman Miller is a company designed by design. And how does this make us different from other companies? We are different, I believe, in how we have managed the company.

Peter Drucker, the foremost thinker and writer on management, defines the term in this way: "Management is thinking through the institution's mission, setting objectives, organizing resources for results, directing vision and resources toward the greatest results and contributions." He goes on to stress, "Without understanding the mission, the objectives and the strategy of the enterprise, an organization cannot be designed."

Charles Eames, asked to define design, said, "One could describe design as the plan for arranging elements to accomplish a particular purpose."

Companies, like products, *are* designed. What has made Herman Miller unique since 1930 is the fact that the designers of our products have also had a vital role in the design of the company itself, that is, in thinking through our mission, our objectives, our direction and strategy. No less important, Herman Miller's designers have been major participants in directing vision and resources to get results.

Initially, D.J. De Pree was at the center of this design. He had studied the furniture industry and found it lacking. He knew Herman Miller, its many weaknesses and very few strengths. He defined the problem and solved it in an innovative way. He made it clear that the designers should study the problems and solve them, and that he would put into production and sell whatever the designers designed.

D.J. became a conduit between the designer, manufacturing, and the market—a unique situation for that time. The design of our business was clear: The designers knew what products people needed, and D.J. and his associates knew how to get them to the market. We are what we are today because of the design of the company for an earlier era.

A designer, George Nelson, gave us our charter. This was a basic part of our design. George's charter reads:

Design is an integral part of the business.

Designers' decisions are as important as those of sales or production departments.

The product must be honest and relevant. It must provide value, function, service. It must be a solution for a living need.

We decide what we will make. If the designer and management like a solution to a particular problem, it is put into production. We have no special faith in the methods used to evaluate the buying public. All that is asked of the designer is a valid solution.

There was an excitement in the air about the changes that were occurring; about the clear definition of needs; about a commitment to innovation and problem solving; about new ideas in literature and advertising and fresh marketing programs. A new vision materialized and a new company was designed.

What form did the design take? Top management was a conduit. Designers were deeply involved. They designed products, and they were also specialists in marketing. They designed advertising, literature, sales promotion materials, showrooms. They were doing what Peter Drucker advocated: They were recognizing needs and setting the direction of the company.

Design had designed a business, but it was not perfect. For one thing, we relied too much on the designer. Management's standard solution for any problem was, as George Nelson complained, to ask the designer to design us out of a problem.

We had great faith in the ability of George and Charles

Eames to solve any problem.

George would urge us to knock ourselves off, but we had such admiration for the designer that we did not want to commercialize his design. We felt that was dishonest. We saw good design and commercialism as polar opposites, and we opted always for good design.

Despite this imperfection, the design, overall, was marvelous. George Nelson was completely involved in Herman Miller. He worked with those people responsible for translating design into production. He was involved in setting marketing directions. He was involved in the strategy of our company.

Charles Eames focused on specific needs, and he gave us a legacy of excellence and quality that carries through today.

Alexander Girard taught us that business ought to be fun, that part of the quality of life was joy, excitement and celebration.

They were all gifted teachers. When I think about Charles Eames today, I think of him as a teacher, more than as a designer.

Speaking of this period, George Nelson said, ''The real assets of Herman Miller at that time were items one never finds on balance sheets: faith, a cheerful indifference to what the rest of the industry might be up to, lots of nerve, and a mysterious kind of interaction that had everyone functioning at top capacity while always having a good time.''

Herman Miller allowed its designers to help shape its policies and direct its energies in a manner unique to American industrial design.

But life had begun to change, both in the market and at Herman Miller.

We had pushed ourselves into fields other than residential furniture. We got interested in contract and institutional furniture. We were beginning to think about the office, and George Nelson designed a group of desks for this market.

Ralph Caplan tells about the scene from the film, *Silent Movie*. Mel Brooks comes back to the MGM lot and is challenged by the guard. Mel says, "Don't you know who I used to be?" We did not want to be known as an organization that used to be. We looked at our company and saw that we were out of balance, concentrating most of our resources on chairs and seating. We had become a chair company.

We could see further that problems and technology were becoming increasingly complex. They were, in fact, creating a different kind of work environment for a new vocational type: the knowledge workers. Their numbers were growing, and the needs of the office had to be redefined.

A representative from the Louvre asked Charles Eames at his Louvre show, "What do you feel is the primary condition of the practice of design?"

Eames' answer: "A recognition of need."

We recognized our need and defined our problem. We expanded our marketing and sales program, shifting the emphasis from design, development and manufacturing to marketing and sales. And we began to achieve a degree of excellence in the office and institutional field. It was still not enough.

We understood and accepted the wisdom found in John Gardner's book, *Self Renewal*. Gardner wrote, "A company that has learned the secret of renewal will be a more interesting and vibrant company, not in some distant future but at once. A company must cause the kinds of change that will enrich and strengthen it, rather than the kinds that will fragment and destroy it."

Our company needed new ways of looking at the problem we were recognizing, and we were ready for new opportunities. We were ready for an accident to happen. Our climate of freedom, our openness to risk prepared us for this accident. We met and joined with Robert Propst, and that produced another major turning point at Herman Miller—a change in direction and redesign of the company. (This change was so vital, changed the company so completely, that I am covering it in a separate essay.)

Designed by design? Yes, and renewed by design, too. But only by designers? Absolutely not. Others, for sure, were contributing to the renewal of Herman Miller, for we had learned that designers were not gods. We as leaders and managers were responsible for the design. So it is not surprising that *design* and *management* mean the same thing at Herman Miller.

Charles Eames once engaged in a filmed interview with a French critic. Because the exchange illuminated design issues so vividly, Herman Miller reprinted the interview as a special flyer. Reprinted again here, Eames' views are no less provocative today than they were twenty-five years ago.

What is your definition of ''design,'' Monsieur Eames?
One could describe design as a plan for arranging elements to accomplish a particular purpose.

Is design an expression of art?
I would rather say it's an expression of purpose. It may (if it is good enough) later be judged as art.

Is design a craft for industrial purposes?
No, but design may be a solution to some industrial problem.

What are the boundaries of design?
What are the boundaries of problems?

Is design a discipline that concerns itself with only one part of the environment?
No.

Is it a method of general expression?
No, it is a method of action.

Is design a creation of an individual?
No, because to be realistic one must always recognize the influence of those that have gone before.

Is design a creation of a group?
Very often.

Is there a design ethic?
There are always design constraints and these often imply an ethic.

Does design imply the idea of products that are necessarily useful?
Yes, even though the use might be very subtle.

Is it able to cooperate in the creation of works reserved solely for pleasure?
Who would say that pleasure is not useful?

Ought form to derive from the analysis of function?
The great risk here is that the analysis may be incomplete.

Can the computer substitute for the designer?
Probably, in some special cases, but usually the computer is an aid to the designer.

Does design imply industrial manufacture?
Not necessarily.

Is design used to modify an old object through new techniques?
This is one kind of design problem.

Is design used to fix up an existing model so that it is more attractive?
One doesn't usually think of design this way.

Is design an element of industrial policy?
If design constraints imply an ethic, and if industrial policy includes ethical principles, then yes, design is an element of industrial policy.

DESIGNED BY DESIGN

Does the creation of design admit constraint?
Design depends largely on constraints.

What constraints?
The sum of all constraints. Here is one of the few effective keys to the design problem—the ability of the designer to recognize as many of the constraints as possible; his willingness and enthusiasm for working within these constraints: the constraints of price, of size, of strength, of balance, of surface, of time, and so forth. Each problem has its own peculiar list.

Does design obey laws?
Aren't constraints enough?

Are there tendencies and schools in design?
Yes, but these are more a measure of human limitations than of ideals.

Is design ephemeral?
Some needs are ephemeral. Most designs are ephemeral.

Ought design to tend toward the ephemeral or toward permanence?
Those needs and designs that have a more universal quality tend toward relative permanence.

How would you define yourself with respect to a decorator? An interior architect? A stylist?
I wouldn't.

To whom does design address itself: To the greatest number? To the specialists or the enlightened amateur? To a privileged social class?
Design addresses itself to the need.

After having answered all those questions, do you feel you have been able to practice the profession of "design" under satisfactory, or even optimum, conditions?
Yes.

Have you been forced to accept compromises?
I don't remember ever being forced to accept compromises, but I have willingly accepted constraints.

What do you feel is the primary condition for the practice of design and for its propagation?
A recognition of need.

What is the future of design?
(The response to this question is a pointed silence followed by the film's end.)

DESIGNED BY DESIGN

Glenn Walters
President, Herman Miller, retired

Directed and led the final design, development and marketing program for Action Office; later Executive President, responsible for U.S. operations; with Carl Frost, began Scanlon '79.

Magnificent years. About '55 through '60 we had some great times. We introduced Charles' products into the mainstream. Before I came, all of the salespeople were either design graduates or architectural graduates, because the product had to be handled with great care and sensitivity. My argument was that if I were a professional salesperson I could still be sensitive to design, but I would know the profession of selling, really a breakthrough idea in a wrestling match.

So I would ask for things like a price on a hundred chairs. Well, they had never sold a hundred chairs to one customer before. We had to go through the agony of learning how to price the product in volume.

I remember a time in 1956 when I had an opportunity to sell fifty desks. So I wrote for a special pricing on fifty double pedestal wood desks designed by George Nelson. Duke Gebben, D.J.'s right-hand man, came back with a quotation that was higher than the unit price of a single desk.

I said, "What's going on here?"

And Duke said, "Well, we don't have the capacity to run that many, so I have figured in new manufacturing facilities which are going to be more costly and tada-tada-tada." I mean it was absolutely wild.

Joe Schwartz

When I joined the company in 1954 in the sales department, there were only maybe a dozen people in sales spread around the company, plus a larger group in New York, Chicago and Los Angeles, where there were "showrooms." Everybody else worked out of their cars or houses or apartments or wherever.

We lived in Atlanta and I think I had originally six southeastern states as my territory. I must have visited every architect who had a doorway. In those days, they were so hungry to see anybody who showed any interest or awareness of the design community. You never stayed in a hotel. They took you home, and you broke bread with them.

You got involved with the colleges and would wind up talking to the students and giving slide lectures on design. Here I was, an engineer who hadn't studied design, and pretty soon I'm a design professor, just by practice.

That is the kind of thing our people today can't find an opportunity to do. They have these big goals, they have to sell tons of stuff; and, you know, architects and designers scare the heck out of them.

My wife was a great devotee, I tell you, of modern furniture. She had traveled during college in Sweden and Denmark and she is really with this stuff. So that in the earlier days every sales guy had a house full of Herman Miller furniture. In fact, my house in Atlanta was my office and my showroom, and customers would come there and we would write orders. You would get out and travel during the daytime and you would come home at night and your wife is sitting there with purchase orders she has been writing up.

Stephen Frykholm
Creative Director

May be best known for his unusual posters designed for Herman Miller's picnics (some are included in the Graphic Design Collection of the Museum of Modern Art in New York); also brought an exciting dimension to the way products and programs are portrayed.

Have you ever gone into a place and just sort of known how to behave? Maybe there is more of that at Herman Miller than we realize. I don't mean a repressive sense, the "ssssh" in the library. But I think there is a code of behavior—in the way we manage or the way we do things—that's a culture. There is a group of people here who trust and respect the talent and the contributions that everybody makes for the good of the whole.

We've often been asked what kind of legacy we will leave our corporate heirs. It wasn't until the company received the AIGA (American Institute of Graphic Arts) design leadership award last year when I started putting together a collection of graphic design work from the late forties to the present day—that I realized the legacy that the Nelson and Eames offices really did leave for me and my staff. They really did establish a set of conditions that have helped us to do the best we could, because that's the way it always had been done.

So the legacy question became very real to me at that point. I realized that, hey, maybe it was their great work that came before us that is allowing us to do it today.

William Stumpf
Designer

A changemaker, making a difference; designed chairs and office systems that gave Herman Miller the chance to develop a new level of business.

Quality is everything. It's that damned simple. It's not winning that's everything. I mean, hopefully, with quality you win. But it's not Vince Lombardi. And that means in every aspect of what Herman Miller does: how it runs itself as a corporation; its relationship with other people; its relationship with the market. It's—when you look at Herman Miller product and you kick it—it's for them to stand up and say, "Yes, we did that."And not hide behind a set of laws, the way a lot of corporations do; or to evade the corporate responsibility that belongs to them.

The second thing is for Herman Miller to be open to the idea—truly open to the idea—of their ultimate vulnerability. That's the key issue. And then be vigilant about that. In my mind, it's more critical than ever in a more competitive world that they accept the idea of what got them to where they are today. The source food of this company is not filling niches in the marketplace. What they need is the thing that keeps great musicians alive, or great architects or great anybodies.

It means the company needs to have a rich storehouse of projects going on all the time. As someone has said, a good editor will see to it that the right things get made. And that you don't ever do anything bad. You may put some things on the market that are good, perhaps, but not great. But never do anything bad; and, hopefully, do some great things.

But what bugs me about the company sometimes—you can't set out to be great. How can anyone tell, while they're doing something, if it's great? How can you tell if you're writing a great book? It's for someone else to decide, isn't it?

Herman Miller's designers have always influenced the direction of the business. Sometimes their involvement was indirect and the result of their reputation. This certainly was clear in our move first into Europe and then into other international markets. The designs of George Nelson and especially of Charles Eames were well known from their earliest Herman Miller days in the European furniture industry and market. At that time, Charles was better known in Europe than in the United States. People abroad who tried to stay on the leading edge of thought and expression not only knew these designers, but also wrote us letters telling us they were interested in our products. Many visited our New York showrooms, and we learned from the showroom staff that European visitors spent hours looking at our products and our program.

By late 1956 the European groundswell was compelling, and we decided that we should investigate. Charles Burgess, then our vice president of sales, and I left for Europe. From the letters we had received, from the records of visits, and from our investigation of the European furniture market, we made a list of the people we wanted to visit. And, as always happens, we added other names as we traveled.

We started in England, visiting some ten manufacturers. We talked to people in furniture department stores and also in the Design Center in London. We also checked the work being done by Knoll, who was then our main competition. Hans Knoll had the jump on us in Europe; he had been born and raised in Germany and had a much greater understanding of the European market and its needs than we did.

We traveled the continent, visiting manufacturers in Holland, Belgium (where, its small size notwithstanding, we interviewed sixteen manufacturers), France, Italy, Germany and Switzerland. We were amazed at the sophistication of the furniture distribution system in Europe—particularly in Germany, where in every large city we found a residential furniture dealer with a large display, an excellent understanding of good design, and well-trained people. They were doing the kind of expert planning for their customers that we wished we had at home.

Where we found people who seemed appropriate for Herman Miller, we explained that we were interested in a licensing arrangement; at that time, there was simply no way we could finance our own way into Europe. Our goal was to find a partner with whom our chemistry was good, someone who also had the financial resources, who had the manufacturing facilities, who understood the European market, and who would translate our design program faithfully.

The last country we visited was Switzerland, and the last people we met with were Willy Fehlbaum and Rudy Pfister. Rudy was there because he was both a good friend of Willy Fehlbaum and his lawyer; he knew a great deal about his business and spoke fluent English. At dinner that first night in Basel, we felt good about these people; in typical American fashion we began calling them Rudy and Willy (something we later learned just wasn't done at that time in Europe).

Before we left Basel, we decided that in Willy Fehlbaum we had found our partner. He was not in the furniture business; his business at that time was store fixtures. He had an excellent manufacturing plant with an integrated process. He was in woodworking, metal working, plating, and finishing. He was eager to work with us. He knew a great deal about our program, had an understanding of good design, seemed to us to be an eager learner. So we negotiated a preliminary agreement with him.

We made another decision while in Basel, about a partner for the United Kingdom: We decided to join with Hille Company in London. They were furniture manufacturers who had their own modern furniture program, with designs by Robin Day. This program was to hurt our relationship later, but we felt at the time that they were the most logical choice for Great Britain.

So following our discussions and negotiations with Willy Fehlbaum, we returned to London and closed a preliminary agreement with Mrs. Hille, her son-in-law, Leslie Julius, and her daughter Rosamond. Both of these agreements were made final a month later during visits by our new partners to Zeeland, Michigan. We had also agreed to appoint a manager who would make sure our commitments to these licensees were carried out. In 1961 we asked Con Boeve, who was then in charge of customer service, to accept this responsibility. He continued to be responsible for and involved in the international program until 1982, when he assumed the presidency of one of Herman Miller's subsidiaries.

As time passed, we encountered unforeseen difficulties with our licensees. The weakness in the licensing arrangement is that the licensee is not fully committed to the licensor. All of our licensees had their own programs and their own businesses. It reminded me of the less than ideal arrangement we'd had years before, when all of our sales people reported to Jim Eppinger: They were committed to him but were not full-time Herman Miller employees.

In Europe, Willy Fehlbaum's dedication and his growing understanding of good design were gratifying, and he enjoyed excellent relationships with our designers. But our dealings at times were stormy. Meetings would suddenly disintegrate into table-pounding and shouting sessions. At times we felt he was unpredictable or intractable in advancing his solution to a particular problem. More than once we parted in anger. One morning in Zeeland, after a particularly difficult meeting the night before, we found that Willy had flown home to Basel. But at other times we found our relationship was as pleasant and fruitful as could be.

We had wonderful times working together with the Schulmans in Paris and the De Padovas in Milan. Fernando De Padova was so committed that he built a manufacturing plant whose capacity, we felt, far exceeded his needs, even in the long-range future. Our assessment proved to be correct.

We enjoyed the tremendous arguments Fernando had with his wife, Madalena, during our meetings. They would seem to launch long, acrimonious tirades against each other in Italian. Then Fernando would sum up for us with a simple sentence like, "Madalena says okay."

In Paris, our affiliated organization was owned and managed by Michel and Theo Schulman, two brothers who were temperamentally as different as only two brothers can be. Usually, however, working with them was not work, but fun.

Working with Hille in London was a different matter. Increasingly, our program and theirs conflicted. More and more, their own designs began to look like ours. Mrs. Hille, the company's dominant force, was a veritable battle-ax. Her father had started the firm, and she took over at his death. Mr. Hille, who changed his name to hers when they were married, worked with the company but was not a notable influence in it. We found that we could deal rather successfully with the couple's son-in-law, but the final decision was always Mrs. Hille's.

One day my brother Max and I were visiting the Design Center on Haymarket Street. Sir Gordon Russell was the director at that time. Walking about, we discovered—side by side in an exhibit—two groups of upholstered seating. One was Herman Miller, the other, Hille. They were so alike that Sir Gordon, visibly embarrassed, suggested that we take some action.

Soon after, on another visit, the Hilles took us to see a copy of Herman Miller products that a competitor was making. The managing director of this firm happened to be on hand. During our discussion with him, he pointed out that some of Hille's products very much resembled ours. Eventually, the similarities between some of Hille's products and ours became so pronounced that we cancelled our licensing arrangements and decided to make our own way in the United Kingdom.

Max and Vern Poest and I agreed with Willy Fehlbaum to form Herman Miller AG, a company owned by Herman Miller and Willy Fehlbaum on a fifty-fifty basis. We had taken one organizational step toward enhancing the Herman Miller program in Europe. The next step, a completely Herman Miller-owned program in Europe, was still years away, not be realized until the early 1980s.

We asked Max to move to Basel to become the managing director of Herman Miller AG. In the negotiations to form the company, we had determined that we should have management control. Willy's son Rolf, who understood the United States and its ways (he was well acquainted with Eames and Nelson and had lived in our home several months), became Max's assistant. Our relationships smoothed out and a great deal of progress was soon made. Max and his family moved to England to begin our own Herman Miller operation there.

Originally, we set up our headquarters for Great Britain in London, but before long we began looking for a place where we could buy or build a factory. A team of management people from the United States recommended Wales. Max then undertook his own investigation and was drawn to the Georgian city of Bath. He felt Bath was a community where our people would be happy, where there was a good labor supply, and where Herman Miller could be a good corporate citizen. We found an available factory in Bath and decided to begin operations.

But Herman Miller was changing, and our associates in Europe were not attuned to this change. As we changed rather rapidly from the residential products designed by Nelson and Eames to office and institutional furniture, our licensees had to find their way in a quite different market.

Their tremendous loyalty to Herman Miller, however, led them to try to enter these markets. Each one did, with varying degrees of success. Fehlbaum and his associates in other European countries were committed to our changing program with their heads—but their hearts belonged to Eames and Nelson.

Our failure to resolve this problem contributed to the need we felt for a completely separate European operation. This was not finally resolved until January 1, 1986, when Fehlbaum took over the Eames products for all of continental Europe. Herman Miller would now control the European market for all of its other programs.

The period of international expansion was a very exciting time. It became a time of growth not only for those of us in senior management, but for many others at Herman Miller as well. There was opportunity for others to travel to Europe, South America and Japan. I think these trips helped to prepare all of us for the growth that we were to experience in the 1970s. Many of us learned a world view that helped to make domestic problems simpler. For me it was not only an exciting time, but a fun time. It gave me and others an opportunity to spend time with our designers, time we would never have taken but for these trips to various countries.

George, Charles, D.J. and I once joined the Fehlbaums and others for a wonderful week of meetings with designers and architects and dealers in Amsterdam, Zurich, Brussels, Milan and Turin. In each of these cities, Charles would speak and show films and George would lecture on design and architecture. In Turin, speaking in Italian, George declared, ''Three great institutions have survived over the centuries—trade, the Church, and prostitution.''

When we arrived in Milan the next day, George was warned by the chief of police not to link prostitution with the Church in his remarks. In typical Nelson fashion, he seemed to agree, but he again made the same linkage before his Milan audience. He got away with it.

THE INTERNATIONAL CONNECTION

I remember a critical time in the mid-1960s in our relationship with Willy Fehlbaum. We were struggling to move from the original licensing arrangement to the fifty-fifty company described earlier. Fehlbaum had his attorneys, we had ours, and we both had financial consultants who had been working with us for well over a year. We finally had a showdown on the train from Milan to Basel. Our discussion became so intense that we agreed to get off the train at Lugano. Willy, his son Rolf, and I walked from the railroad station to a small park overlooking Lake Lugano. We sat down on a bench, with Rolf between us. We palavered, Willy speaking German, I speaking English, and Rolf doing instantaneous translations. We were not going to move from this bench, we had decided on sitting down, until we had solved our problems. It was one of the most interesting and exciting negotiations I have ever taken part in. And we solved our problems!

It is my belief that if we had not gone to Europe in 1956—and, of course, if we had decided then not to expand into the international arena—Herman Miller probably would have remained a relatively small company with low, easily achievable goals. But because of the influence of Nelson particularly, and of Eames, I doubt that we'd have stood pat. George and Charles were not going to let us languish in Zeeland, Michigan. There was never any disagreement, anyway, in the top management on going international.

And so Herman Miller's mandate for many years has identified the company as an international organization, though Herman Miller's name had been fixed firmly in Europe long before that. And indeed we are international, with major facilities located in Toronto; Bath and Chippenham, England; Croissy-Beauborg, France; a regional office in the Middle East; with licensees and dealerships all over the free world.

BUSINESS AS UNUSUAL

Con Boeve
President and CEO, Miltech, a Herman Miller subsidiary

Led Herman Miller's international program for many years; has
a talent for understanding the various cultures and thinking of
Herman Miller's associates around the world.

*The thing that was terribly important to me in all those years
were the many relationships developed more on a human cove-
nant than a corporate basis. I think we have to understand at
Herman Miller, for posterity, that you don't muck people about.
No one can say what the design integrity of Charles Eames was.
How do you write that down and make it live?*

*I remember in 1967 we had an international conference for
our licensees and, really, it was of no significance to Herman
Miller. I suppose in the context of the company's long-term interests, we had some responsibility to these people, maybe thir-
teen or so, from the continent of Europe, South America and
Japan.*

*So we brought them into New York. We had this marvelous
fall morning. We were in the St. Moritz Hotel overlooking Central Park. I had a breakfast set up 'way on the top floor, and it
was gorgeous. We spent time in New York at the George Nelson
office and the showroom, went to a Broadway show, then we
flew out to Chicago and we bussed them all up to Zeeland. Point
West was just in existence at that time, and we had really good
meetings in Zeeland.*

*Then we went to Santa Fe to see Girard, and Girard hosted the
whole group for dinner. It was unbelievable. We took them out
to a little Indian pueblo, and there was a potter named Maria
who only potted this black clay. Oh! People bought some of that
stuff and it's worth a mint today. I mean, you can't buy a piece
of that for under a thousand dollars. It was incredible.*

And then we went on to Eames in Los Angeles.

*The whole point of my saying all this is just to reflect on what
I recall as some of that Eames mystique. I had to go out there
ahead of time. In fact, I ran the whole course before and set up
this thing within the pueblo, too, and everything 'way ahead of
time.*

*Anyway, I went to Eames and we sat on a blanket outside of
his office eating strawberries in a setting that I didn't know quite
how to relate to, because I was out of a little different cut. But
I sat out there with Ray and him, and we figured out how we*

were going to do this thing. I had to go up to his house, and I had to walk to where the bus was going to be; I had to find out how we could get the bus to the right place, and then we had to make a certain entrance because he was going to serve lunch at his house.

It was billed as "A Day with Charles Eames." We started out in the morning at Twentieth-Century Fox Studios. They had a little champagne, a coffee break, you know. He, of course, had that all set up beautifully. And then we went up to his house for lunch. You walked into the house and looked out to the yard, where he had this big circus tent up. And he had white tables and red and blue chairs, you know. Eames chairs. And he handed out little sunglasses—red, white, and blue stripes. It was just unbelievable.

So then we went down to his studio. Whenever you went to his studio—and I had on a few other occasions to do it—it was always like, oh, you just happened to drop in sort of thing. But there was never a thing left to chance. Anyway, we went through his studio and he showed us all his fastballs in his slow way, and everybody was just overwhelmed. Then he set us down in a little theater and he started to introduce some slide shows. He showed us this marvelous show about his trip to India, and this show and that show. Then he said, "There's one more little show that I think you would like to see."

The day before I had taken these people to Disneyland. Eames had a photographer or two that he'd put on the bus with me. And Hugh and Max were with us at that point. But anyway, this photographer just took a million pictures of these people at Disneyland.

I had had some pictures taken as well, which weren't too good, even though I hired good people to do it, at the previous stops on the trip. Just as soon as this film would be exposed, I'd send it to Eames. But all of a sudden this shed that's his studio just resounded with a stereophonic "Stars and Stripes Forever." I mean, it just blew the roof off that place. And here on the wall is a three-screen projection going on covering the U.S. trip—including Disneyland—of all these people who were sitting there watching.

They had stayed up all night, those Eames people doing those slides. I'm telling you, it was just the most amazing thing. They cried, those licensees. They literally cried.

The legendary tales of Rohde, Nelson, Eames, and D.J. are so entertaining (and we do prefer legend to fact), that it is often easy to forget the effect that the events and people of the 1960s have on the Herman Miller of today. The huge impact made by the flow of fertile ideas during those years—the years of Bob Propst, the inventor, and Herman Miller, his champion—produced the fourth and most influential turning point in our lives.

(I must explain why I have reached the fourth turning point before acknowledging the third. Turning points one, two, and four—The Rohde, Nelson-Eames, and Propst eras—were generally of a piece: They have determined the design and direction of Herman Miller. Turning point three was of an entirely different nature. Through a personal experience of D.J.'s, combined with the influence of Dr. Carl Frost and the Scanlon Plan, the principles of equity and justice for everyone in the company were introduced and nurtured. The story behind turning point three will come later.)

It was about 1955 when we started to move into the office market. Sales and marketing groups were reorganized, for we recognized that these areas had been our weak point and thus would need increased strength if we were to continue to grow. Although we were still pushing our residential program, our designers were contributing less and less to our needs in this area. George Nelson and Charles Eames were broadening their own interests, and they seemed unable or uninterested in studying and solving our problems as they had in earlier years.

During those preceding years, the most important design and product development work had led to the horizontal expansion of the Eames chair program. We had a wide range of chairs filling a variety of needs. Some sales people recognized this; they also saw the difficulties growing in the residential field. So they began rapidly to expand our sales in chairs. Management adjusted. We offered lower prices, better discount programs, and more sophisticated marketing and sales tools. We became a chair business.

This was fun. It was simple, it was profitable; but it wasn't long before we were fretting about what would happen if the bottom fell out of our chair business. We were vulnerable. We asked our designers to design us out of this problem. They tried but did not.

We had a new kind of major crisis, one we had never confronted before. And we were definitely open to chance and change. Enter Robert Propst.

Our years with Bob Propst began this way. D.J., while visiting my brother John at the University of Colorado in Boulder, decided to see a local architect named Hobie Wagner. Wagner was out of town working in Minneapolis with a client. So D.J. strolled about the drafting room visiting with people in Wagner's firm. He asked them if they knew of anyone doing interesting working in the area. One of them told him about a young man in Denver.

D.J. phoned this man, Robert Propst, and arranged to see him the next day. He took the bus to Denver. "He came down and we sat around in our ginky place—truly ginky—and we had a great visit," Propst recalled years later. "I knew something about Herman Miller but had no interest in the furniture industry, except that I knew D.J. was a notable person."

D.J. was so excited by this meeting that he phoned me and strongly suggested that I meet Mr. Propst. We met later at the Aspen Design Conference. It was a memorable time. Our chemistry was so good that it became obvious we had to work together. We were then in the middle of forming a technical center, so our first discussion raised the possibility of Bob's joining us as its director. However, as we talked further and exchanged ideas by mail and phone, it became clear that together we could do much more than simply manage a tech center. We needed a better arrangement.

Seeing Bob's shop in Denver, listening to his description of a litter and hospital bed project he was pursuing, reviewing a variety of other projects which he had in mind —all of this opened a new world to me. To solve our crisis at Herman Miller, we needed new thinking, new ideas and the kind of development work that Bob Propst wanted to do. We agreed that he would work part-time for us: twenty weeks during the year beginning September 1, 1958.

Bob's ideas ranged far beyond furniture; these, we agreed, we would work on later. We immediately embarked together on projects related to our business. On September 19, we decided to move forward on four particular projects: a spring cushion development, a furniture mold process, a "Plant #1 case study," and certain hardware projects.

The project list began to grow, mostly with ideas that had little or no relation to furniture. The first year and most of the second was a time of excitement and joy: of visions of a new Herman Miller, of interesting and detailed discussions about joint ventures, one with a company making seats for exotic new military jet planes. But it was also a time of worry and frustration because our resources were not sufficient to cope with all of Bob's projects. We became even more concerned when our limitations led him to consider other business connections. One of these seemed so good that he decided to cancel our agreement.

This we could not accept, for our vision of a different Herman Miller was becoming clear. We would continue in the furniture business, but we would diversify through the projects Bob was developing. We valued the talent he could bring to the company. We thought our relationship could be fruitful for him and us alike. We needed him and we were confident that he needed us. Whether we could afford each other, however, was an open question.

"We didn't have any money," Vern Poest confessed later, "but Hugh and I went up to Denver and met in Bob's barn and worked out a deal with him. So we got the thing set up and we took our chief financial consultant, our chief auditor, up there one day. I won't mention his name, but he is a very noted man in financial circles today. Coming back, we had lunch and this gentleman said, 'You guys are crazy. You are just putting the money down a rat hole.' He said, 'In my experience, you will never come up with anything out of an investment like that.'"

Vern has since reflected on this remarkable turn of

events: "Is that foresight? Or is that luck? Or is that providential?" And his answer: "I don't know."

We agreed to take a giant step and form a research division designed to expand and intensify the company's commitment to *the pursuit of diversification, to innovation, to meeting human needs, and to expanding the leadership role for Herman Miller.*

This research division would define problems and propose solutions directly pertinent to the furniture operations. It would propose products for development and manufacture by Herman Miller. It would propose new products that could be developed through us and brought to the market through either a new division of the company, a joint venture or a license to other appropriate organizations. This division would be responsible not only for the development of new product ideas, but also for the continuing development through manufacture and sales and marketing.

In September 1960, we announced the formation of a research division directed by Robert Propst, to be located in Ann Arbor, Michigan. We asked Glenn Walters, then in charge of companywide marketing, to join this division as business manager. He would be responsible for the continuing development of new products through manufacturing and to the market.

To our board I reported, "This division represents a definite move by Herman Miller towards diversification—a long-term interest in expansion in the general area of living, as distinguished from the present primary furniture efforts."

We began with thirty-two projects under development. Our enthusiasm for diversification is illustrated by a range of prospective products that included a waffle spring, a roof system, an energy clamp, a heart valve, a squash ball caster, a livestock identification program, and a laser projector.

Our mandate for research was to propose products and

programs that would enable us to diversify. We asked the new division to stay out of the design of furniture; for that, we would rely on Nelson and Eames.

In setting up shop for our new research division—even before moving to Ann Arbor—we asked our planning and design group to design the offices. They did, using our Comprehensive Storage System (CSS). Bob Propst was very frustrated, not only with their solutions, but also with all other products available to him. His ability to see the problem quickly and his curiosity took over. Our early agreement that provided him a climate of freedom to pursue problems on a broad front enabled him to move outside of the restrictions we had placed on research. It seemed at the time that we had made only a minor decision when we did not object to his working out the problems of establishing these offices.

Bob began to concentrate largely on the way people should work in the office. He consulted with behavioral psychologists, with architects, mathematicians, and anthropologists. He quickly discovered that the problem was larger and more exciting then simply the design of furniture. He defined the problem: How can we enable people to work more effectively and efficiently? How can we assist them in maintaining health, interest and joy in working in the office?

It was this study that enabled Bob Propst to delineate clearly the basic propositions which later came to be incorporated in an interior system which he called Action Office. From this study, the research group was able to design its own offices; not content with that, they built prototypes which they installed and began using.

Then, instead of doing what we had learned to do best—the "wrong" thing—we took a step backward and did the "right" thing. We assigned the design of Action Office to George Nelson and asked Bob Propst to return to developing programs that would enable Herman Miller to diversify.

CRISIS, CHANCE AND CHANGE

As Bob and Glenn Walters reported progress on their thirty-two projects, we were intrigued by visions of a diversified company moving far beyond the furniture business. Laser beams, heart pumps, sugar-beet thinners, and tree harvesters were much more interesting than the rather staid furniture business.

Action Office was on the list of thirty-two projects, and we knew it was there. But we did not know the extent to which Bob himself was continuing to pour his own thinking and energies into it. This was to cause conflicts in the future, but we did not foresee them then. For while we were immensely interested in the research, we were also working closely with George Nelson on *his* designs for Action Office.

Within a year some light began to dawn for us. A docket of thirty-two projects was unmanageable. We were drowning in complications. We found that to sell an idea, it had to be developed more completely than Bob thought it needed to be. We were overextended and could not commit the necessary resources. Seeing this, we began to focus and concentrate our efforts more effectively on Action Office. We urged the Nelson office to move faster.

We were beset by conflicts, some a shade below the surface, others roaring loud and clear. Some people in management occasionally dragged their feet. Glenn Walters, the one charged with helping to make something happen, spoke recently of those days: ''If you're really committed to innovation, it's a lonely condition; because, while your organization may be attentive to innovation, innovation is by nature threatening. And you build organizations in a way that you don't want them threatened.''

Outside board members were not enthusiastic about research, but the most serious problem centered on what we had always considered our strong suit—design. George Nelson and Charles Eames disagreed with our direction and goals for the research division. George suggested once that we discontinue the operation. In March, 1962, at a meeting in Ann Arbor, he indicated an interest in just two of the division's many projects: Action Office and a development called the Generated Roof Structure. He was utterly bored with everything else.

A few months later Charles Eames wondered why research did not work on real problems, like lighting. He suggested an exchange of ideas but thought anything beyond that impractical. He said we were too concerned with innovation, a position he held until his death. He suggested using the money we were spending on research to build service and quality—another subject he would hammer at during our entire association.

At another meeting, we reviewed an operational chair on which Propst was working for General Electric. George was unwilling to discuss it; because General Electric was his client and his territory, he resented the intrusion. At one point, however, Charles and Bob worked together on the design of the chair. They were unable to see it through.

But these spats and conflicts were resolved, and the rallying cry was usually "the interest of the company." Following one session, George wrote to Bob, "The kind of stimulation that could come from a more lively interaction between us is something I would welcome, for it cannot help benefitting the company." We even tried to merge the research group into the Nelson office, but the idea failed for lack of support.

By early 1962, it was obvious that change was needed. We examined and reaffirmed our objectives and goals for research. We defined the problems. We issued a "restatement of purpose," slashed the project list to manageable size and reorganized to accomplish what we now felt we could do. But the development of Action Office remained a no-win situation.

The Nelson office was designing Action Office and consulting with Bob Propst and many others in Herman Miller. On one meeting with Nelson and Propst, my notes read: "We discussed Action Office. We related this to the

CRISIS, CHANCE AND CHANGE

Comprehensive Storage System, thinking that the components of Action Office could be incorporated within CSS. We talked about seeing Action Office as 'performance in the office,' not as furniture; about setting up clinical displays in showrooms where we could handle businessmen's needs on an individual basis.''

Within a year, the Nelson office had designed this product, and in 1965 we introduced Action Office 1 to the market. The media, dealers, architects and customers thought the concepts were innovative, exciting and a new way to see the office. The designs were beautiful and the various elements—desks, storage units—worked well, looked and even felt good. We designed an extensive publicity program. We interviewed about thirty public relations firms and told them exactly what we wanted: articles in certain magazines, stories in *Saturday Evening Post* and *Business Week*. We selected one firm that did everything we asked and more. It was a successful launch.

Initial enthusiasm was high, and we appeared to have a new solution for the office. In Bob Propst's view, however, these designs did not reflect the concepts he had started. We agreed. The feedback from our salespeople was that we had produced "another marshmallow sofa''—a product that was beautiful and exciting, but didn't work. Of more immediate concern, though, was the difficulty we were having with making this a quality line. Many parts were hard to assemble. Costs were far too high. We could not afford die castings, so we made sand castings. The pieces, individually or together in an office, looked elegant and rich. But the design was not complete. Action Office 1 did not live up to Propst's concepts.

Some thought it a case of poetic injustice when George Nelson won the Alcoa Award for the design of AO-1, because no mention was made in the award of the basic work that had been done by Robert Propst.

From the beginning of the development by the Nelson office, we had planned two versions of Action Office. With the "Executive" version introduced, I defined an economy version yet to be designed by September, 1965, in these words: "The economy version to aim at a different market. Middle management-scientific oriented. Half the cost. Must satisfy all factors in AO concept. To consist of a limited number of highly tooled integrated components assembled with simple tolerance connections. Must work both as individual desks and as part of office landscape or mobile wall."

Our directive declared, "The Nelson Office, Research Division and Product Development are responsible for this development. They must now translate the criteria into a product system."

We had solved one problem, ever so clearly, but once again were hung up on the past: The Nelson office had to be the designers. Friction between the Nelson office and Propst's research division began quickly with product development trying to act as the referee. Each group was working on a different basis, with very little interaction. Finally the Nelson office proposed a system based on the use of large one-piece molded parts, while Propst proposed a system based on a limited number of tooled parts which could be assembled with simple connections.

At a tense meeting in New York, we began to see some daylight. Bob Blaich, the company's design director, and I decided that we would begin a three-month competition with each group developing its own proposal, following which we would make a choice. As so often happens, in the end, we did not have to make a decision. The Nelson office did little to develop their thesis. Propst, at the deadline, had his completely worked out. We chose Propst's because it was logical and doable.

Now we were moving. The research division had been reorganized. The project list was smaller, and we had begun to abandon our dreams of a highly diversified company. We knew there was potential in AO. The responsibility for it had been assigned. We were in focus. And

Bob Propst and his associates swarmed into the problems.

We seemed so close to the reality of a new system. So much work was being put into it by a sizable number of keen and committed people. But we soon discovered that we were bogging down in an ironic problem: too many ideas. Every time a design problem seemed to be solved, research would figure a different way to do it. We realized, then as always, that there is no way to reach perfection—but still Propst and his team tried. Much as management encouraged and even demanded completion, it didn't happen. The research group was prone to explore, not complete.

They should have heeded Charles Eames' dictum: "If you make it as good as it can be by next Tuesday, it's probably as good as it can be." But they did not—especially Bob Propst.

In September, 1967, I attended a seminar in Chicago organized by Carroll Cihlar and sponsored by *Office Design* magazine. The subject was "Open Plan in the Office." I found it surprising and scary that a few others were finally thinking about the office as we were.

After all the years and effort we had put into Action Office, we could not let someone else take what we had learned and beat us to the market. Quickly, we had to figure a better way to organize the development work and provide the resources to reach the market. We had to take away the primary responsibility for the development from both design and research, but still keep them involved. This would be a huge step away from our historic position regarding designers. The designer, we had always insisted, studied the needs, solved the problem. Our responsibility was to bring the product to the market. And our relationship with Bob Propst had been built on the same premise.

We had already taken design responsibility from the Nelson office. Now we made another decision: The Nelson office would no longer have *any* responsibility for Action

Office. Research would be involved but not primarily responsible. On October 3, 1967, I assigned the responsibility to Glenn Walters with this letter:

It is now more clear than ever that we must organize carefully and quickly for the introduction of Action Office II. We must make the following assumptions:
1. Completing Action Office II is the most important problem facing Herman Miller today.
2. Problems to be solved before we can introduce it are in Design, Engineering, Manufacturing, Costing, Controls, and Marketing. These need the first hand attention of top management in each of these fields.
3. I, therefore, assign direct responsibility for completing the product and introducing it to the market to the following task force: Glenn Walters (chairman), Bob Blaich, Dick Ruch, and Steve Snoey.
4. Your goal for introduction is Spring, 1968.
5. Primary responsibility for this product has been in Research. It is now your responsibility.
6. You have as resources all the people who work for you. In addition, Bob Propst, Max De Pree, and Vern Poest are ready to be used as resources whenever you need them.
Your task force has the authority to work out all facets of the completion and introduction of this system. Progress reports, however, should be made periodically. May we have the first of these on November 1?

On October 11, 1967, Glenn Walters issued this call to Action Office personnel:

Attached is a copy of Hugh's October 3 memo setting up a task force on this project.
An assignment of personnel has been developed by the task force in line with the attached list. [Forty-four people were given specific assignments.]
Our first briefing session will be held Wednesday, October 18, Administration Building and will consist of:

CRISIS, CHANCE AND CHANGE

1. *Review of the Propst concept*
2. *Review of hardware*
3. *Discussion of individual areas of responsibility.*

A statement of Marketing Strategy is attached.

Glenn scheduled the mid-October meeting to launch the project for 6:00 P.M., and people were traveling that day to make it. I had been in Los Angeles working with Eames and arrived at O'Hare too late to make my connection to Grand Rapids. I ran into Tom Pratt and learned that he had chartered a small plane to fly himself and four others directly to Holland. There wasn't room for one more, so Tom insisted that I take his place and he would follow on the next commercial flight. (The weather was stormy and I would have preferred to take the commercial flight myself, but Tom knew I should be at the meeting on time.)

Five of us boarded the plane, including our public relations consultant Carl Ruff, and the graphics designer John Massey. John arranged for me to sit next to the pilot because I'd had some limited experience as a pilot. This plane had two engines, one forward and one aft, prompting John to call it "the flying bicycle."

The pilot was dismayingly young—all of nineteen, I would guess. As we taxied to the runway, he kept looking back. I asked him why. "Just checking to see if the rear propeller is turning," he said.

We received our takeoff instructions, and he unaccountably turned off the radio as we took off into the darkening autumn storm. I was unhappy with no radio contact and asked him about it. He said he didn't realize that it was turned off and agreed that he would need it for departure from the Chicago area.

We climbed to about 3,000 feet and headed directly across Lake Michigan. Belatedly, we learned our pilot was not qualified for instruments. The clouds ahead forced us lower and lower, and each time we descended another few hundred feet the waves below us loomed larger and angrier. Finally we skimmed over the dunes at South Haven and our fledgling pilot set us to searching for landmarks to navigate by. Nearing Holland, I was obliged to issue instructions and a course for our approach and landing.

Scary, you bet. But John Massey's wit and our enthusiasm for the meeting just ahead tempered our fright and made our trip in the flying bicycle memorable.

Beginning the meeting, I emphasized the importance of this work by making an extreme statement. It is true, as sometimes quoted, that I told the task force, "You can do anything except sell the company to reach this goal."

Glenn and the task force calculated specific percentages of time they expected from each of the forty-four members. A checklist covering eighty-nine activities was discussed and assigned. The marketing strategy statement proposed a goal of five and one-half million dollars in sales annually two years after introduction. (It was an excellent goal, of course, but far under what we actually achieved. What a wonderful mistake to have made!) Those who attended this session will probably never forget it.

We were finally off and running on a project that would change our lives, change Herman Miller, change the industry—and even the way people everywhere worked in offices.

For the next ten months, the challenge lifted our spirits. The intensity was exciting, and in July 1968 we introduced Action Office II with the first seminar in the Union Bank Building, Grand Rapids. The greatest of changes had begun.

Robert Propst: An Innovating Force

Soon after Action Office was on the market, Bob Propst published *A Facility Based on Change,* the book that raised interest and provided support for Action Office. To try to give readers, customers and Herman Miller people an understanding of this man, I wrote the following preface:

CRISIS, CHANCE AND CHANGE

"In 1958 we at Herman Miller began to feel the need for adding another dimension to our search for problems and problem solutions. We were beginning to identify this as the need for research as part of the design process, when, at the Aspen Design Conference we were fortunate to meet Robert Propst. Bob Propst had been an artist, a sculptor, a teacher and an inventor. His thinking, his talents seemed to mesh naturally with our needs. So after a period of consultant relationship we formed the Research Division of Herman Miller with Bob Propst as its director.

"Our first directive to him was to find problems outside of the furniture industry, and to conceive solutions for them. He immediately began flooding us with ideas, concepts and drawings, ranging from agriculture to medicine. It is interesting, though, that despite our mutual desire to explore other fields, the first project that attracted his continuing attention was the office, and as early as 1960 he began outlining his concepts for this activity. The first step in the evolution of the products resulting from this study was introduced in 1964 and the second step is now being presented.

"Bob Propst has brought to Herman Miller the new dimension we felt we needed. His ideas are always exciting and often controversial. He had the unique ability to study a problem thoroughly and almost immediately to begin arriving at solutions. He is a firm believer in the team concept. He is a conceiver and initiator and it is a tremendous joy to work with him to complete his ideas."

But that only begins to describe Bob Propst, his influence on Herman Miller, and his impact on those of us who worked with him.

In my essays on design, I discussed the turns that have changed Herman Miller. The perspective of history enables us to see that two of these turns made Herman Miller a completely different company. First there was D.J.'s study of the industry, the coming of Gilbert Rohde and the change to modern furniture—all of which resulted in a radically changed company. Second, Robert Propst's thinking forced us to see ourselves, not as traditional furniture manufacturers, but as a systems company that was providing a better way of working in an office.

The Herman Miller we see so clearly in 1986 was not even dreamt of in 1968. Nor could it have been, because the force at work within the company was true innovation. And while true innovation can take you on a marvelous journey, it cannot tell you when you will arrive or what your destination will be like.

Bob Propst was the innovating force behind a remarkable journey. To portray the journey best, I must describe the force behind it—the kind of person Bob Propst is and what it was like to work with him.

Bob grew up on a ranch in Colorado. He is the first to acknowledge that it was the extraordinary climate of freedom during his childhood that whetted an insatiable appetite to try things. He recalls that he and his brother could do anything "as long as it didn't cost anything." A great believer in the importance of play as an ingredient in problem solving, he also credits childhood labors in retrospect for arousing a curious intelligence. "It was a life of terrific drudgery," he says. "So it occurs to you that the whole business of getting the beets out of the ground and topping them ought to be mechanically assisted. I had some thoughts even as a little kid on a mechanized way of doing this, and when the way turned out, to my surprise, almost exactly what I had been thinking about, I thought, 'My gosh, I should have done something about that when I was a kid.'"

The contradictions of discipline, the need for improvising, the freedom and openness of the range country all influenced him—and still do.

"My life was really crazy," he once told me. "I went off to school to be a chemical engineer, and in midstream—this friend of mine was taking design and he said why don't you take a design course? So I took a design course.

CRISIS, CHANCE AND CHANGE

Right in the middle of my undergraduate education I changed to a fine arts major. It's interesting that maybe that is one of the things that happens to people who get into creative activity—a strange rupture in the midstream of education. You go clear into another department and you find that they don't believe in any of the things your former department believes in. You stop believing in all disciplines.''

World War II started and Bob became a beachmaster in the South Pacific. He recalled later, ''You go ashore after the attack wave gets on the beach, and then there you are. It's without a doubt the world's most incredible case of confusion: trying to manage a totally unmanageable situation, making incredible decisions and then watching all kinds of tremendous consequences immediately afterwards. I think it was the world's greatest training ground for innovation and development, because after that experience everything looked less difficult.''

And perhaps it was, for after the war he and his wife, Lee, started and organized an art department at a junior college in Texas. Then as now, it is worth noting, Lee Propst has been a full and vital partner in the Propst family's professional life. For that matter, so, too, have been the Propst's four children, who worked during the Ann Arbor years when, as his staff remembers, the research program was one great extended family.

In Texas, the Propsts spent two years inventing art courses at night and teaching them the next day. Then Bob went back to the University of Colorado for his master's degree and headed the extension division of the university's art department. ''I really had a great time teaching,'' he has said. ''And then I developed the idea—and this finally became a passion—that the artist needed to be more involved functionally in society.''

He started a small architecture-sculpture business in Denver. Starting from zero, he called on an aircraft company, a major lumber company and a pre-cast concrete company. "I made a crazy speech. You are not going to get innovation from your in-house pals. You know that. You don't know how to stop building airplanes and do other things with your technology. You need another kind of thinking."

Soon he was involved with these and other companies and their problems. And that's about the time D.J. visited him in Denver. Then I met with him in Aspen, and soon after that we began our relationship.

Our involvement with George Nelson, Charles Eames, and Sandro Girard and the association with other architects, designers, and artists those three brought into Herman Miller activity had changed our lives. Our work was exciting, and we had learned much. Now after those first meetings with Bob, we felt a new tinge of excitement. We were amazed at his completely different vision, his wide ranging interests and insatiable curiosity. Before us was the possibility of an entirely new way to look at problems, and we were not disappointed.

Our ready commitment to work with him proved to Bob that we were open to new ideas—not welded to Nelson and Eames and their designs, thinking and leadership. Since we were willing to work seriously on projects that had little or no relation to our business, he concluded he was with people whose attitudes and resources would enable him to grow and develop his ideas. This was firm basis for our long association and was the glue that was to help carry us through the major changes that occurred.

Bob Propst was not a designer. "He never liked the word," recalls Bob Snyder, who as a university student was the first person Bob hired to work for him in Ann Arbor. "He is more inventor or researcher. But he didn't like the 're' part of researcher either, because that meant you were just looking backward, instead of forward. He liked 'searcher.' It is interesting that we never subscribed to design magazines. The office literature was not magazines like *Industrial Design* or *Progressive Architecture.* Bob said, 'Anything you see in there has already been done.' So we'd get the *Wall Street Journal, Forbes, Harvard Business Review,* maybe *Psychology Today. Scientific American,* I think, was a great favorite of Bob's. I think the only things he liked to see that were already done were at home in the Sears catalog. When Bob and Lee used to have me over for dinner, there'd be this sort of fireside ritual of lying on the floor and thumbing through the Sears farm catalog. I am sure it carried over from his early days on the ranch.''

When a new idea struck Bob Propst, the sparks would fly. But then he'd strike more new ideas before the old sparks died. He was seldom distracted by sparks, because he could so clearly see the problem and then define the solution. Often, his interest in potential technology helped him to discover appropriate methods and technology, then connect these to problems.

He was quick. His is a mind that works continually, never seems to rest. One of his closest associates at Ann Arbor, Jack Kelley, says, ''Bob could articulate the problem. Most people can see a problem, but he could articulate what the problem *was.* Once that was done, it was pretty easy heading toward the solution of that problem. That was where he was marvelous, doing that.''

As a rule, Bob Propst's ideas come not from some rationally ordered thought process, but from a personal encounter. This is somewhat at odds with his social inclinations. Bob Snyder says, ''I would never call him outgoing. He did not believe in the business lunch or large cocktail parties. If you went out to lunch in a group, that was to get your mind off the work and onto something else. He felt you might find something else out there through a fortuitous encounter.''

Snyder recalls that while Bob avoided large social affairs, he was never afraid to strike up a conversation with a stranger. ''As a matter of fact,'' says Snyder, ''he wrote a neat little essay on how to ride an airplane and learn something. It was about how to stand in the boarding area and pick an interesting person to sit next to. He was intrigued as much by someone in coveralls as he was by someone in a three-piece suit.

Whatever the circumstances, Bob Propst was always doing applied research. For example, while he was a patient in the University Hospital at Ann Arbor, he conceived and drew the essential outlines for CoStruc, Herman Miller's product system for hospitals. Even though it took us almost ten years to bring this to the market, the basic concepts changed little from those he created as he lay in the hospital.

Once the toilet in the research office became clogged with a discarded sanitary napkin. With a plumber's friend, Bob fixed it, then immediately designed a new sanitary napkin—a four-part device that would break up quickly.

Many of Bob's early ideas, such as the cattle identification program and the sugar beet thinner, came from his experience on the ranch. He saw a problem in building and related it to a new technology, the laser beam. He designed a laser unit that would keep a structure level during the building process. That was in 1962. Later, a company working in that field reinvented the process.

Action Office was conceived as he confronted his own needs for work space in the small building we had rented in Ann Arbor for the newly organized research division. He was disappointed that while Herman Miller was in the office furniture business, there were no real solutions to working in the office. That was typical: He was usually dissatisfied with conditions as he experienced them. It follows that working with him, or for him, ranged from joy to agony to joy, sometimes in a ten-minute span.

Those who were not supportive of his ideas or his way of thinking found their personal relations with him tenuous. He believed his way was the right way, and usually it was. He asked for support, not blind loyalty, but did in fact work best with people who saw solutions as he saw them. In the development of the locker for CoStruc, for example, he solved the back assembly one way, but our engineer group solved it a different way. This became such a huge issue that I was asked to resolve it. The engineer's solution was better, but Bob and I had to meet in Grand Rapids to discuss it. He suggested that he might resign—his solution was that important to him. In the end, not only did we agree to use the engineer's solution, but the experience also strengthened our relationship.

Bob, like Eames, made huge demands on his associates. He understood the abilities and talents of each, and by his own example forced others to work far beyond their own inclinations. His mission in life was to act on a concern about people and the way they worked and lived. But he did not always extend these same concerns to his own group.

Again, like Eames, who had a Don Albinson or Dick Donges to aid or abet his work, Bob needed someone who could get things done: to convert his ideas, which were often unfinished, into reality. In short, to execute the design work. Almost from the beginning, Jack Kelley was catcher to Bob's pitching. Without him in this role, little would have been accomplished. Joe Schwartz was another key person. He had been assigned responsibility for bringing Action Office to the market. He was a man who had the unique ability to immerse himself in a project and give 100 percent of himself to it. He and Jack were the kind of talent Bob needed. As bear catchers, they translated ideas into products and services. They forced Bob to concentrate on priority projects—something difficult for him to do—and they provided the connections to reality that finished the job.

Throughout our association there were doubts about Bob Propst and his ideas. Some people had a "suspended philosophy" and believed we should return to designs of furniture like the classics of Eames and Nelson. Bob's answer was, ''I have no argument with that, but to me it's irrelevant. While it's great to get your mitts on a great piece of furniture, it's bad to be saddled with design ideas that may in ten years be way behind the values and needs of the time.''

Others could not accept the freewheeling process practiced at research. Bob wanted Herman Miller to concentrate on his projects and could not understand the allocation of funds to designs which he believed did not fit Herman Miller's direction. Such intensity was deeply resented by a few, and they sometimes tried to subvert his programs.

Joe Schwartz was not one of those subversives. ''Propst was really a terrific guy; we had a lot of fun together. He used to come to my home for dinner, and we'd talk and he'd get so mad. 'Damn this company,' he would complain. 'Why don't they buy my ideas? You know, I should go somewhere else with my tree harvester and my farm irrigator . . .' He would go on and on.

''I would sit and listen to Bob in sheer amazement, because Nelson and Eames were dormant, Girard had already retired, and one hundred percent of the products that Herman Miller was producing were of his invention. And here he was complaining.

''I said, 'Bob, you've got to look at it differently.'

''He said, 'What do you mean?'

''I said, 'Look, if Eames and Nelson and Girard were active and vital and producing and delivering proposals to management, like you are, management would have to make a selection out of a broad number of proposals from all these designers.' I said, 'As it is right now, you've got a one hundred-percent market share. What more do you want?'

''He used to look at me and shake his head. 'Well,' he would say, 'that's true. But I'm still not happy.'''

But as with Nelson and Eames, his vision and commitment to his ideas had a strong impact on the design of Herman Miller.

CRISIS, CHANCE AND CHANGE

Why was Bob Propst successful with Herman Miller? He saw in this organization the strength and eagerness to introduce ideas ahead of their time. He needed a champion, and we provided that. He needed wheels to carry on his projects, and we had those wheels. He could not identify the quality of freedom in any other organization.

Involvement with Bob meant that almost everything else was boring. The scope, possibility and potential in his ideas made the process as exciting as design can be. He raised the level of thinking and perspective for many and challenged people to see in a larger way than they had thought possible.

Early in the vital work of the task force, the rethinking he forced on us of how we managed margins and costs and how we produced products changed the manufacturing process. He insisted that AO be not precious, but a system that served people at work. His impact was felt beyond the shaping of products, services and systems. He also influenced attitudes and stimulated many, many people to think and to carry their thoughts far beyond their own expectations.

Long before the term squat team was coined, Bob Propst and I contrived to have a memorable one. With the success of Action Office, Herman Miller began to change rapidly. Both the company and Herman Miller Research were struggling to keep abreast of growth, and we urgently needed time for thinking and planning our future. But we found it so difficult to arrange meetings that Bob and I decided we had to isolate ourselves for intensive discussion of both corporate and research problems.

We found a large basement room that was normally used for staff meetings, and during the week of February 7, 1972, we took it over. We gave notice that for that week we were to be left alone. We set up shop with a large table, two chairs, two blackboards, an easel with a large pad of paper, and plenty of wall space.

We called our project "Goals and Direction for the 70s."

We began to exchange ideas and to talk them through. As we did, we wrote and drew them on the blackboards or pads. Every time an idea got expressed on the pad, we would tear off the sheet and stick it to the wall. We began work every day at eight in the morning and continued until evening; and more than once we returned for more work after a quick dinner.

Day after day, we took a hard look at ourselves, our corporate state of health, our life signs. We reviewed our history and asked each other what it meant to us, what we felt should now be expected as a result of this history. We wrote out tangible objectives, priorities and directions. We discussed how we could keep out of the whirlpool, that murky center of organizational problems, and so stay at the leading edge. We discovered, where Action Office was concerned, that we had been thinking only of a hard product and concluded that an information product was missing: To protect our system hardware, we agreed that we needed aggressive information delivery.

And so it went. By Friday night the walls were covered with notes, drawings, cartoons and vast amounts of scribbling.

Finally we issued a book, *Notes on the Structure and Direction of Herman Miller*, based on our squat-team efforts. We gave a copy to each of our officers and many managers as a guide for the 1970s. For Bob Propst and me, this document became a bible for thinking about who we were and where we were going. I believe it was used in much the same way by those others in management who were responsible for Herman Miller.

Robert Propst at Herman Miller was a generator of creative tension which moved us farther than we thought possible. His enthusiasm was so visible it permeated the organization. His far-ranging interests were frustrating and exciting. His ideas and concepts, supported and expanded initially by a small group and then by many others, changed our lives: They changed Herman Miller, changed an industry, and changed the way millions of people work in the office, the hospital, laboratory and factory. He left us all of that, and a legacy of research.

Bob Propst made a difference.

BUSINESS AS UNUSUAL

Bob Propst

The first real agreement we had with Herman Miller was that we would work on problems of the living environment and what effect they may have on the productivity and satisfaction of people—which is about as complicated as it ever got, really. Of course, all the disciplines were very sketchily connected to this, as they are even now, and there was no research format of any kind. There were no concepts of measurement or evaluation of any kind. No experimental premise. So this was a fantastic bootstrap effort to start from zero and create a whole format to do this.

We finally picked Ann Arbor to be closer to a lot more resources. A big university like the University of Michigan was used to dealing with the outside world, and it was 140 miles from Zeeland, which stopped too many casual involvements. So it turned out to be one heck of an interesting premise.

We were always on what amounted to a sundown relationship with Herman Miller. If we didn't propose projects each year that they were interested in sponsoring, we did not have a relationship. We were never employees of Herman Miller. We also cut a deal that we had to have leeway to delve into areas that might seem completely outside their area of interest— agriculture and material handling, waste handling, areas of communication, building structures—because those all seemed like elementary things.

So that started a very long period, four or five years of sort of plowing around in all these disciplinary areas trying to find out what was happening: A lot of new things in behavioral sciences, a lot of new things in the human factors world were coming forward. We were in all kinds of bags. We were always the strange persons at conferences. And we looked into new materials. We spent a lot of time with people like DuPont. What were the new synthetic materials going to be able to do? And could we compel and drive them toward more interesting performance, rather than taking an exotic new material and trying to do something with it that wood could do? Should we try to find some whole new uses for materials applied to intelligent solutions, rather than materials running around trying to find an answer, an application?

As we began to develop embryonic ideas of how we might function in these areas—new kinds of products, new ways of producing them, new kinds of manufacturing—we were also considering the antiquated way of manufacturing and delivering furniture structures: Building boxes, shipping them out, never having anything in inventory. Wouldn't it be interesting if you actually had product in inventory? Wouldn't it be interesting if we could machine tolerances where we didn't have to assemble the cabinets? Where we could ship without ten or fifteen percent damage before the product ever got to the customer?

We gradually developed an experimental format. One of the most interesting projects was tracking down the way super performers—the really gifted, productive people—do their work in a different way. We interviewed people like Margaret Mead. In some cases we had to do it almost by espionage—finding out how Dr. Emory Land works, or Kelly Johnson at Lockheed. We spent a half day with Steve Allen, who is a very productive person, a very nice person with marvelous insights.

Hy Bomberg

My daughter studied Chinese, and I learned a fascinating word from her. The Chinese word for crisis is made up of two ideograms. One of them speaks of danger and the other one speaks of opportunity. So crisis is a combination of danger and opportunity.

Of course, Herman Miller for years was a premier design-oriented company. Action Office changed that. There was a tremendous reaction against it. People couldn't understand this whole concept of open plan. When you mentioned open plan, one had an image of this great mass of desks with curtain screens and plants. Managers and the people who would have to work in these environments were saying, "No way. I don't want any part of that."

What they were seeing was office landscaping. What they didn't understand was Bob Propst's philosophy—that the sense of selective enclosure gives one a wonderful balance between the need to be private and the need to be involved, to be a social animal.

What is particularly interesting is that very little has changed. Very little. We've become more sophisticated in our awareness, and we have better documentation of the things Propst was maybe intuitive about. But everything he said then is even more valid today: the rate of change, the technological breakthroughs, the awareness of human factors. All of these are even more valid today.

Glenn Walters

You would hope that in every organization there is organizational ambivalence, just as there is human ambivalence. I can remember the time, for example, in Ann Arbor when Hugh brought Bob Propst and me together to set up the Herman Miller Research Corporation. He told us that he wanted to diversify the business and that we could do anything we wanted to do. There were just two no-no's: One, we were not to get involved in anything with warlike characteristics because he just never wanted this corporation to be dealing with armaments. Second, we had to stay out of the furniture business. That, he said, was all taken care of by Charles Eames and George Nelson and Alexander Girard.

Well, of course, Bob Propst by that time had thirty-five or thirty-seven projects, all of which were non-furniture as specified by Hugh. I mean, although he had some furniture elements like a waffle spring which could be a generic part of a seating system, nothing was actually furniture.

In setting up shop—even before going to Ann Arbor—Bob Propst was very frustrated with the kind of equipment that was available to him, including all the Herman Miller products. To make a long story short, we ended up getting into the furniture business but in a different way—through Action Office.

Nobody wanted Action Office. There were only a few of us. Hugh said, "It's going to be done." And so we said, "Yes, sir." He appointed a task force and put me in charge of it and said, "Do it." He gave us a time line and we did it.

But there was great argument. The sales force at that time was absolutely ridiculing that decision. Our budget to move that product into the marketplace was $25,000—most of the marketing-sales budget in 1968. And sales wanted that $25,000 for advertising Eames chairs and tables.

This was something new. It was untried. It was untested. It was innovation—something so foreign that they were scared stiff. And they would have the responsibility for selling it. And what did Charles say about the product? Well, one of the things that Charles said is that it is "honest ugly." What greater indictment! Right?

What would I like the people at Herman Miller to remember? It was the agony of that singular decision. It was not a spontaneous, automatic group-think result. And it wasn't the logical step-by-step way—with good strategic planning programs, good five-year plans, good one-year plans all in sequence, all handled appropriately by planning directors with the music in the background and we're all singing, "Hail! Hail! Hail!"

This was a massive fight. The manufacturing area, for example, was a major battleground. The product that was manufactured up until that time was fondled. I apply the word to the work force. It was fondled by the work force. You've seen the Eames rosewood chair. In the manufacturing process, the workers would literally fondle the parts with a great deal of sensitivity.

And so, when we went to Action Office, we had to deal with an entirely different market—new attitudes in regard to volume and cost-price relationships. It had to zip through—zip-zip-zip-zip-zip. And the work force would say, "But this isn't Herman Miller quality. If I can't fondle it, it's not quality."

That's an indication of the fantastic commitment we had to the design ethic, and everything it implied. As you know, making change, getting behavior modification, is extremely difficult.

Like Eames and Nelson, Bob Propst needed catchers who were able to field his ideas, understand them and convert them, often unfinished, into reality. These people I call bear catchers and skinners. They were maze bright. They needed and had authentic management skills. They sought responsibility, were problem solvers, had communication skills and resource keenness. They had special talents for translating ideas into products, systems and services. They forced the designers to concentrate on the priority projects— something usually difficult for an innovator to do—and they provided the connections to reality that enabled the designers to finish the job.

It would be a most unusual innovator or designer who did not need bear catchers close to him. Innovators are described in one of Dr. Seuss's books as those "who go beyond Z." That talent enables them to think, to conceive, to articulate new ideas. However, with the initial draft of the idea spelled out, they often assume the problem is solved, and go on to something else. Then, to everyone's surprise, a contradiction rears up, and the flow of ideas from the designer continues to expand and alter the already clearly defined concept. This can be exasperating, for it means delay and confusion while myriad improvements or detours along exciting but barren routes are explored.

So the bear skinner's goal of driving a project to reality was usually frustrating, and those people who were closely responsible wore out quickly, or, with the education they had received, they moved on to less demanding or more responsible positions where they were often able to make outstanding contributions.

J ohn Pyle and Ernest Farmer understood George Nelson. They were part of the design process and provided the necessary refinement. At the same time, Bill Staal contributed the practical know-how to the production process that made the object of a design easier to manufacture.

Duke Gebben carried the burden of the detail and operations. He knew the needs in the factory and understood how he could support D.J. He was D.J.'s bear skinner.

Without the work of Don Albinson, Dale Bauer and Dick Donges, the work of Charles Eames would have been incomplete. Eames needed people who knew what he was trying to do, and by proposing alternative design solutions, these men enabled Eames to develop his ideas.

From the beginning of the research division, Jack Kelley was the bear skinner for Bob Propst. He and an increasing number of others gave a great portion of their lives and thus enabled us to bring to market the programs which changed the lives of so many.

Pep Nagelkirk's ingenious ideas, the innovative way he executed them in three-dimensional form, and his wonderful sense of excellence made him a most valuable bear catcher—first for Nelson and Eames and then for Bill Stumpf and Don Chadwick.

Others helped immeasurably. Call them intervenors, translators, explainers and connectors. They all contributed to the process of conception, design, development, engineering, production and marketing of the exciting innovations that came from Herman Miller. And their role became more necessary as the complexity of the ideas, the process and the organization itself grew.

There have been giants in Herman Miller, and such people will continue to be drawn to an organization which gives them the freedom to innovate. But without their associates, who both caught their ideas and used their special abilities to make direct connections to reality, we would have been a quite different company—at worst, like those businesses which act as gatekeepers for the privileged few, where only the ''in'' people may enter, and where only ideas that benefit them alone are allowed past the gate.

But Herman Miller would not be the kind of company it is today without the unique contributions of thousands of others—those bearers of responsibility, those people who made it happen, those who designed the tools and machines, who made the products and designed the services needed. People become owners of this business through their ideas, their influence, participation and that portion of their lives they devote to it. Such ownership is passed on from one generation to the next, and it becomes an inheritance from those who have gone before and built the basis for the way we work together. Our connection to those bearers of responsibility can be felt by a look at a few of those people who exemplify an endless line of splendor.

Nick Baker was the engineer who literally provided the fuel on which the factory ran. When a shutdown occurred, Nick was there to get things going again. He shoveled coal, kept the boiler pressure up and made sure the central machinery on which the plant depended was in top shape. He would put the boss's sons to work cleaning the boiler during summer vacation, and his whole body vibrated with delight when I would emerge from inside the boiler covered with soot.

Ray Schaap was the shipping clerk with an unrelenting sense of urgency. If the last piece for a shipment was delayed, he would roar up the elevator shaft, ''I want that 3930 dresser down here in five minutes or I'll come up and finish it myself.'' He was the perennial emcee at the company picnics and never failed to limit D.J. to ''a few minutes'' when he introduced him.

Otto De Jonge was a furniture finisher spraying lacquer on dressers and chests. He usually had a gripe about something, but he worked hard and, during the Depression, willingly walked nine blocks to work for only two or three hours. He didn't drag out the work to make it last longer. He worked as hard then as he did when times were better.

Hugo Larm was the quiet cabinet room foreman. He spoke softly but had complete skill and know-how; and he knew his people well. He had the authority of competence and used it wisely.

Alvah Loring helped organize the upholstery department when we began making modern chairs and sofas. He did the tough jobs, and until he retired he made every prototype that Nelson and others designed. He was always impatient to begin the day. With feeling and understanding, he taught many of us how to upholster. Alvie gave dignity to work and insisted that the details were most important in his craft. He was the first man I knew who could chew Copenhagen and spit tacks at the same time.

Ella De Vries was a sewer in upholstery. Her cheerful, easy attitude and her drive for quality seemed to be contradictory traits. She easily endured the fun-loving group in this department and helped Carl Frens, the foreman and a stolid Dutchman, to cope with the free spirits.

Andrew Johnson was a master finisher and one of the few "color" men in western Michigan. Andy knew that he was good and would occasionally use the fact that we needed him to ask us for more money. Off the job he dressed with a flair. He was a dandy who resembled Michigan Governor Van Wagoner. At one picnic several people believed he *was* the governor and had come to speak. Andy did nothing to discourage this notion. At the beginning of the Scanlon Plan he provided pertinent information which helped in formulating the bonus part of the plan.

Gene Kroll was an enjoyable and diligent man skilled at packing furniture. Years ago, he and I bet a chicken dinner on the World Series between the Yankees and the Dodgers. The Yanks won, but despite reminders for years and years, he did not pay. Then in one of those magic moments at my retirement dinner, he presented me with a Colonel Sanders chicken dinner—one of the few moments of that event that will be remembered.

Gerrit Schreur was responsible for molding plywood for Eames chairs. This was a technology that had no history. Eames had designed and built the presses we used. He called them ''kzamms'' because when the plies were put in and the pressure applied—*kzamm*—out would come a seat for a dining chair. Gerrit quickly developed the skill to adjust to the variety of conditions present, the mysterious changes in wood, plastic, climate, and the perverseness of the kzamms Eames had invented.

Ken Duthler was that rare combination: a doer and a teacher. He was the top salesman at Herman Miller for three years, a ''cube'' winner for many more, and had the ability to teach others how to do it. He used every hour and every opportunity to accomplish his goals. He once arranged a visit for us with Governor Clements of Texas. Shortly before we were ushered in, he learned that the governor had ordered all thermostats to be raised to save energy during the hot weather, and that he did not like ties. Ken told us to remove our ties, and in we marched. Ken was wearing a dark blue suit with vest and stiff white shirt with French cuffs. Governor Clements shook Ken's hand and observed, ''They really got to you.''

Clare Hintz was responsible for the Herman Miller textile program from its beginning until he retired in 1972. He was a creative craftsman who combined technical knowledge of materials and processes, understanding of textile design, and experience in marketing and sales with managerial talent.

With nonstop enthusiasm he defended, promoted and supported Alexander Girard in the design of the textile program. A conversation with Clare convinced one that textiles were our principal business, Sandro Girard our only designer, and that our fabrics set quality standards for the entire company.

He told us endlessly about Scottish cattle eating only the lush green grass, never touching barbed wire, and growing the finest leather "best auch" in the world.

Clare had almost too much ability and willingness to move ahead independently. He once decided Girard's fabrics should be used for ties, and before I knew it he took us into the tie business. We quickly decided it was the wrong business for Herman Miller, but I am still wearing those India silk bow ties.

Jim Eppinger and D.J. were the only two people about whom this could be said: "Without him this company would have disappeared." Jim was D.J.'s Aaron, an eager, able, hard-working young man when he joined Herman Miller. With the coming of Gilbert Rohde, he quickly understood the future of modern furniture and what it could do for living in the home. He arranged office space in Rohde's office and began the redesign of his life to conform to his commitment to this new furniture. Jim and Rohde hired me after graduation from college. The experience was priceless. I learned something about design, but more importantly, I learned from Jim a great deal about hard work, commitment and loyalty.

Jim organized the first showroom in New York. He persuaded the Wanamaker department stores in New York and Philadelphia to allow Herman Miller to build twelve rooms in each store, fill them with furniture and staff them with people he selected. This was an unheard of direction for these conservative, successful department stores to take. Jim's title was sales manager, but he was so much more. He was involved in making the arrangements with Nelson, Eames and Girard. For a time he financed the work of Charles Eames and arranged the relationship with Zenith Plastics, with whom Charles worked out the design and manufacture of the first plastic chair. Jim was in charge of sales, but he also performed as the connection to designers. He was our first product manager.

Occasionally, D.J. and Jim would argue vehemently, mostly on railroad platforms as the train was leaving Kalamazoo or New York. They always seemed to put off these fights until the end of a visit. These were very serious confrontations, for they had nobody else to challenge their ideas—and these were ideas that had to be fought through. They were two men held together by their belief in what they were doing, their ability to perform, and the respect they had for each other.

Jim Eppinger was totally immersed in the company. He was part of the program that changed Herman Miller and changed the home furniture industry.

And what more can be said of all those others who, along with the people I've mentioned, accepted continuous change, understood the need for such change, became committed to it and made things work. And it continues today, as you can see in the workers' views of the development of Ethospace, Herman Miller's newest array of products. Here are a few reactions:

"When I saw a new product line coming up, I wanted to be part of it. We've had to sacrifice to put it in place, but that's what makes it fun—the challenge of trying to figure out what's wrong and how to fix it. It makes you feel part of the team."

"It's a new frontier, a new adventure."

"You have to come in with the attitude of change every day."

Such people, like many before them, are bearers of responsibility.

D.J. has told the story over and over: "It was in 1927. I got a phone call one morning at seven o'clock, right after the factory day started. Herman Rummelt had dropped dead. He was a millwright, and a very good one.

"So I visited his wife that morning. The first thing she did was to take me around the house and show me the handcrafted things Herman had made. They were all nicely designed and very wonderfully executed.

"Then she came in with a sheaf of papers, and this was the poetry that he had written. Then she told me about the night watchman we had who was in Rummelt's department. He had been a machine gunner in World War I and had killed a lot of Germans. He thought he was a murderer and was going to Hell. She told me that her husband spent hours between the watchman's rounds sitting with him with the Bible to show him there was reconciliation and forgiveness of sins.

"I walked away from that house that morning rather shaken up.

"Later I attended the funeral, which was only a block away from Rummelt's house, and the pastor read some poetry. Well, walking home from there, God was dealing with me about this whole thing, the attitude toward working people. I began to realize that we were either all ordinary or all extraordinary. And by the time I reached the front porch of our house, I had concluded that we are all extraordinary. My whole attitude had changed."

There is something of a parallel between D.J.'s profound realization that working people are all extraordinary and his recognition that the products of his company must be as fine as design can make them. In both instances, the fulfillment of D.J.'s strongly felt need depended on people and forces beyond himself or his company.

So it happened that a fortuitous encounter—providence—once again changed the direction of Herman Miller. In October, 1949, D.J. and I attended a meeting sponsored by the Grand Rapids Furniture Manufacturers Association. The speaker's topic was "Enterprise for Everybody." We were deeply affected by his thoughts about labor and management relations. On the way home, we decided we had to learn more about what we had heard, and that we should ask the speaker to help us.

Shortly thereafter we visited this man at Michigan State University. He was a member of the faculty. Rather naively, as we soon found, we proposed that we hire him to install at Herman Miller the plan he'd outlined in Grand Rapids. We were dumbfounded when we found it was not that simple. Instead, he began to ask questions about our ability to manage the business.

Were we open to the ideas and suggestions of everyone? Were we willing to share information about the business so that others could become involved in it? We left our meeting without a decision, but he did agree to visit us in Zeeland. He did, and picked up where he had left off— asking those of us in management the same kind of questions. He also visited with many people in the factory and finally agreed to work with us. He agreed to install the Scanlon Plan.

We soon realized that once again we had found a giant: a changemaker, a questioner, a teacher, a person who made a difference. His name is Dr. Carl Frost. We all soon came to know him as "Jack."

Jack Frost began to teach us that the Scanlon Plan— named for Joseph Scanlon, once a professional boxer, cost accountant, labor leader, teacher and theorist—is an innovative strategy for managing an organization. It is innovative in philosophy and innovative in structure. It is participative, with formal committees to involve all employees in the decision-making process. And it is innovative in compensation, through a productivity sharing bonus.

We learned through Jack Frost that the keys to this plan were these:

People throughout the organization have to be individually identified as resources who can accomplish the objectives of the organization. But that means management first has to identify those objectives and be willing and able to translate them to these people.

People then have to have the opportunity to participate, to question, to initiate, to be innovative, and to become responsible.

People need equity; therefore, Herman Miller needs an understandable way of sharing the financial benefits that will accrue through participation.

And so a change began, a change that was satisfying but irritating, rewarding but frustrating; a change that brought us all closer together but also brought about occasional doubts. It was a change from ''piece work'' and every man for himself to each person being not only responsible for himself but also for every other person in the organization. ''Get off my back'' was heard often, but we soon began to understand that we could help each other.

It was never easy, but it has been worth it!

Screening and production committees met every month to study and act on suggestions. Through these sessions, people were informed about the opportunities, problems and plans for the business. Management began to learn a better way of managing, and many, many people accepted the responsibility of contributing their ideas and influencing the decisions that had to be made. During the Scanlon Plan's first ten years, we averaged one suggestion per person each year, and the bonus averaged ten percent. The belief grew that this was the best way to manage a company.

We could not understand why this plan didn't sweep through industry. At a Conference Board meeting, I once proposed the idea to the head of a business with 35,000 employees. ''Arch,'' I asked, ''what could you do with 35,000 suggestions every year?'' His response was that his company was profitable enough. What he really meant was that he did not want to manage that way.

Has the Scanlon Plan changed the understanding and commitment of people to the business? I think so. People need to be needed, want to be productive, need to be responsible, have the right to know, need and want to own the problem. The plan can answer such needs.

Does management have to abdicate some of its responsibility? No, but the plan does demand increasing skill by management, particularly in communications and in identifying those people who can be key resources on specific projects. It does force management to define the direction and objectives of the company, and to translate them to everyone. Then it can be seen by everyone that there is a direct relationship between management performance, profit, people involvement and bonus.

The entire organization wants to know that management is working and performing. One month in 1972, we suffered a surprising twenty-five percent loss because of poor scheduling. At the next screening meeting, one of the elected members said to management, ''You guys messed up.''

The Scanlon Plan increases the opportunity for a business to make an impact on society. It teaches people to care, to be concerned with what goes on around them. One of the needs of society is to be involved in successful operations. Scanlon is an innovative way, a tool for fulfilling this need. It raises the level of understanding and commitment within the business and teaches people how to contribute to the community and society. In the same synergistic way, the expectations for higher productivity, improved environment and better quality can in turn set higher standards in the communities we serve and, beyond them, for society in general.

PEOPLE AS BEARERS OF RESPONSIBILITY

As we learned to live with the Scanlon Plan, we found that it had to be both flexible and all-encompassing. The first version, adopted in 1950, was specially designed to meet Herman Miller's needs. About 120 people worked for the company at that time, and ninety percent of them were production workers employed in Zeeland. For the next quarter century the plan remained essentially intact, with only occasional adjustments.

By 1977, however, we realized that the plan needed a major overhauling. Almost 2,500 people now worked for Herman Miller in several locations in the United States and in Canada and England. In particular, the bonus provisions which were primarily fashioned to apply to production work were no longer responsive to half the employees' job situations—those who did work which was not directly related to production.

I believe the process through which the company's people modernized the Scanlon Plan remains today a model of corporate democracy in action. In early 1978, Glenn Walters and Jack Frost met with all U.S. employees of Herman Miller. Everyone was asked to answer these questions by secret ballot:

Is there a need for change? (ninety-eight percent said *yes*)

Is there potential for improvement? (ninety-eight percent said *yes*)

What's in it for you; what are you looking for at Herman Miller? (fourteen percent said *job security;* twenty-nine percent said *personal growth, challenge, and opportunity;* ninteen percent said *more money*)

Would you volunteer to be part of a change process? (ninety-six percent said *yes*)

Such positive support led to the election of fifty-four people to an ad hoc committee representing nearly every segment of the company. Three subcommittees were formed: Education and Communications, Rules and Regulations, and Equity. A key management person was appointed to lead each group, and several additional financial specialists were assigned to the Equity Subcommittee.

The ad hoc committee worked on a new structure for Scanlon for almost ten months. As reported by the committee, this structure would do the following:

Provide specific procedures for planning the company's performance.

Identify annual performance commitments from employees against which they would be measured.

Establish a new structure which would encourage all employees to define and solve problems that hinder meeting the needs of customers, investors and employees.

Establish a system to monitor performance.

Expand the bonus calculation to more accurately reflect all employees' performance.

What became clearer than ever, the committee concluded, was that "Scanlon is more than a bonus incentive plan; it is essentially a way to manage the business."

The committee's long and deep immersion in its task produced a sixty-page proposal for the company's consideration. They named it "Time to Learn about Scanlon '79," and that is just what everyone at Herman Miller did. The proposal included an outline for a new Scanlon structure of work teams, caucuses and councils, together with a new suggestion system based on this structure. Much food for thought.

The first step toward approving the ad hoc committee's proposal was getting understanding, acceptance and commitment from the executive committee. Next came the other executives and director-level managers—division by division.

A number of amendments and revisions were offered by

the various divisional leaders. After some discussion, the changes were accepted by the ad hoc committee and written into the final draft presented to the company as a whole on January 10, 1979.

After this general introduction, employees received details of the proposal in small group settings. Discussions were led by ad hoc committee members or those who had been trained by the committee members.

Finally, on January 26, a vote was held, simultaneously, in all company locations across the United States, among all employees. They voted by over ninety-six percent to accept Scanlon '79.

An enormous collective effort had achieved a notable goal. "In a great many aspects," says Judith Ramquist, one of the ad hoc committee's most energetic members, "we were redesigning the company. But in the same way, what the company had become was redesigning the Scanlon Plan."

There can be no doubt about it: The Scanlon Plan is a living part of the design of Herman Miller today.

Dr. Carl Frost: Always in a State of Becoming

"Do you know what day it is?" "What are today's realities?" Dr. Carl Frost—who often asks these questions, who designed the Plan in 1950, and who has a unique way of encouraging, nurturing and prodding—has made sure the Scanlon Plan fits the realities of today. Once again, the story of a company and the difference it can make was changed by the advent of one person who has perhaps enriched the quality of work and life for more people in this business than anybody else.

How did one man affect our lives so much? D.J. once said of Jack Frost, "He taught us all we know about the humanities of a corporation—a priceless ingredient." (And I will talk more about what this meant to the business in the next essay.)

Jack spoke often about the need for understanding, ac-

ceptance and commitment. He practiced that with fervor.
From the beginning, he studied to understand and know
the company and the people, and his commitment to all
of us carried us along. His persistent yet gentle way of asking questions—he was always asking questions—enabled
him not only to gain acceptance but to learn from many of
the troubles, difficulties and snags, the details of the business. We had confidence in him and liked and trusted him.
By the same token, Jack had boundless confidence in the
capacity of people to excel. In a paper on the Scanlon Plan,
he wrote, "Too often scientific management has frag-
mented the job into meaningless elements. Industrial engineers have been commissioned to engineer the human
factor out of the job. The management, the foreman and
the standards police the job, disciplining the people. Have
you ever thought of the potential when people react to
challenging competition, assume their responsibility for
quantity, quality and costs—disciplining all the factors
within their situation to perform their jobs?"

He concluded, "Once the people know the job, the exciting demands of the customer, the strengths of the competitors and the costs within their control, they have got
a focus on their target. They may not always hit the bull's
eye, but they will score!"

No wonder the people care about Jack as a person. In
1952, as everyone at Herman Miller has heard, people
were concerned about his driving "that old wreck of a car"
from Lansing to Zeeland. They said among themselves,
"This man needs a new car. Couldn't we manage this if we
all pitched in?"

So the morning came when a new Buick stood in the
parking lot. All 120 employees joined in. Jack was called
out of the factory and the keys to the car were given to him.
The employees themselves had hatched the whole idea
and paid for the car with voluntary contributions.

Jack once told an interviewer, "We have found that the
people who have successful Scanlon companies are more

informed about more issues, more informed about their own kind of job, the product, and how their corporation fits into the point where it's conspicuous to other people. I think the Scanlon kind of people don't live in quite as flat a universe as do other people.''

The knowledge he collected through his friendly questioning enabled him to serve anyone. His way was both to ask questions and to make suggestions, but never to tell you how to do something. Through two long assignments in Brazil and Nigeria, he continued to influence our lives and the way we worked. In 1965, he wrote me: ''Are you learning to add up the pieces of experience into more comprehensive solutions? Is Glenn showing signs of maturing into more objectivity in his personal relations so that his professional competence can be used effectively by other people? What evidence have you seen for the growth of the production echelon of your organization? Are they asking questions regarding their work and the company? What concrete accomplishments have they experienced to give them reinforcement and reassurance of their importance?'' Such questions and the suggestions behind them reminded us of things ignored or undone and forced us to think them through and act.

Jack's emphasis is always on performance and productivity as keys to the well-being of the organization and the business. He taught that without these, there would be no joy in work or in business. He influenced us far beyond the Scanlon Plan. For each one of us, he has been someone to whom we could go with any problem, sure that he would not only listen but would help.

For management, he was often like an office chair that would not swivel—an irritant that forced correction and change. He served as a spur, an advisor, a confessor. We often asked ourselves, ''What would Jack think?''

Once after an intense working day in Basel, Switzerland, I went for a long walk. I had anticipated enjoying a quiet evening alone. As I passed a small café, the aroma of cheese floated around me. It was a restaurant specializing in a variant of fondue called *raclette*. I loved cheese fondue but had never tried *raclette*, so I decided to eat there.

I entered a small room filled with people sitting at wood tables on old wood benches. The scene resembled dinner time at the Herman Miller picnic in miniature. German only was being spoken, and the air was filled with this marvelously strong smell of melting cheese. I thought of walking out—I'd told myself I wanted to be alone—but I did speak some German and therefore was quick to understand I was being invited to join the group for dinner.

Then and there, I experienced perhaps the most instant change of my life: one minute alone and the next celebrating with people I had never seen before. As we ate and talked, I felt these people cared about me and were willing to share their good time with me. Their companionship renewed and lifted my spirits. It was not much different from the way we helped each other in our Scanlon screening and production committee meetings, where we first began to learn our need for each other, and to see that we were responsible for each other. Just as those Swiss people that night cared for me and felt a social responsibility for me, so in those early Scanlon meetings did we learn to care for each other—to learn that we were all bearers of responsibility.

PEOPLE AS BEARERS OF RESPONSIBILITY

Vernon Poest
Senior Vice President, retired

Brought the reality of profits to Herman Miller; led the change from a privately to a publicly held company; as Chief Financial Officer, ensured the financial resources needed for growth.

We're always hearing that you've got to be a "people" company. I guess Herman Miller's known as one of the big people companies, whatever a people company is. As I look back, from a non-people, financial/engineering perspective, I would guess that we're a better people company than any other company I know of. Scanlon, for us, has been a remarkable tool. It was a philosophy, but it was also a tool. It was a philosophy of how people interacted in a business, and that was always said to be the major part of Scanlon. The bonus system was secondary to the interaction, handling people, their interaction, their being able to manage their part of the business. That was the major part of the package.

I've talked to Jack Frost for hundreds of hours over the years; he was my friend and consultant during the mad sixties and seventies. Great guy. He would always say that the philosophy was the most important part of the plan, and that the bonus sort of got tacked on to the bottom of it. On the other hand, it's always hard to get a unifying force unless it's something specific, like dollars and cents.

I can always talk to you about the budget, and you and I can always absolutely understand. But if you start talking about philosophical things, or feeling about people, what this people company is—then we've got problems. And yet this little bonus system tacked on the end sort of tied the whole thing together. The performance of the people tied into a reward for the performance that everybody participated in.

Now, we had problems over the years, because the company changed. And it changed so radically and so fast that we fell behind at times; we had to have makeups and pickups and changes in compensation systems and changes in organization. That was not because the Scanlon plan philosophy wasn't good, but because our company was changing so fast. There was nothing that stayed static. Nothing.

Through the years, it's been tremendous. From a management standpoint it's been very difficult. For you to have to go out to monthly meetings and have to answer questions about—

*whatever. Like, what are stock options, and why do some peo-
ple get them and some people don't? Well, most managers
would never in the world want to face questions like that, and
yet that's what we're doing as a matter of course.*
    That kind of concept was, and is, a beautiful concept.

Edward Simon
President, Herman Miller

Designed Rapid Response, a program offering fast shipment of
basic Action Office items; has a history of accepting major
challenges and solving key problems; as Chief Operating Officer, is both a thinker and a doer.

*Everything that is done in Scanlon is done to produce an eco-
nomic result, period. But there is a higher value here at Herman
Miller, and that is the fundamental people orientation—the
fundamental value of a person that transcends Scanlon. I don't
think Scanlon leads us. I think we have been able to take Scanlon and use it for participative ownership as a result of our fundamental belief. We are saying there is an investment of an individual's life in this company, and for that investment a person should be able to share in the equity of the business—in the
growth and value of the business.*
    *I think that Scanlon is better today. Participative ownership
is better today. And it is better because of the contribution made
not only by the spirit of the De Prees but also by the spirit of the
non-De Prees. It is one thing to preach a set of values, and it is
another thing to be able to live with the promise of a set of
values, from the equity standpoint of the workers. If there isn't
organizational support and commitment to economic justice for
the worker, and if this view is not shared by the rest of the
management team, then nobody can drive it through in a company of this size.*
    *So I think the values of the company have grown immensely.
I really believe it is the perseverance of management at each
step that is making Herman Miller a better company. There are
foundations that are laid by each successive group, and so it is
a better company today than it ever was. And it will be a better
company five years from now; it will be a better company ten
years from now than it is today.*

PEOPLE AS BEARERS OF RESPONSIBILITY

It is a transfer of values, nothing else. It is really making sure that there is continuity of management. That continuity has to be a thread running right to the board of directors, so that we make sure, over the passage of time, that one can see whether or not we have people who really have the values or just pretend to have the values. One cannot fake it over a long period of time.

You see, the worker knows. You will never fool the worker. Management never fools the worker. If you can't talk the business intelligently to them, then they won't talk to you. If you believe in that, and if you can do that, then you will get people to call you and say, "I'd like to talk to you. Could you come to this meeting, could you do this or could you do that."

But you will never fool the worker, and the only reason why you know that is because you have been a worker yourself. I'm not saying that has to be the case for everyone, but I think a manager really has to understand what it is like to be the under-dog, just how hard it is to do factory work. It is hard work.

Richard Ruch
Senior Vice President

Began in finance, then assumed responsibility for manufacturing and administration; now back in finance as Chief Financial Officer; understands Herman Miller and its people; leader in the Scanlon Plan for many years.

We have had a participative management process at Herman Miller for more than thirty-five years—long before participative management came into style. We define participation as the opportunity and the responsibility each employee-owner has to be included in the decision-making process to the level of one's competence and job responsibility.

Participation is not permissive. It requires competence, discipline, and commitment. We believe participation enables us to achieve above-average results. Douglas McGregor once said, "We cannot force people to work for management's objectives." But through participation we can improve personal commitment to business results.

At Herman Miller, ownership is more than just psychological. One hundred percent of our full-time regular employees with one or more years of service in the United States are stock-

BUSINESS AS UNUSUAL

holders. When this program was introduced in 1983, Max De Pree said, "I believe it is significant that all employees in the company are stockholders because it is synergistic with the participative management process which we have had since 1950." Max went on to say that employee stock ownership is a clearly competitive reality—nothing is being given. Ownership is earned and paid for through the Herman Miller profit sharing plan, which has been in place since 1970.

There are three values connected with ownership: business literacy, equity and spirit. To fully carry out our responsibilities as owners, we must be literate in our business. We expect a knowledgeable, professional team of people who understand the values, goals and operation of our business. For participative owners, this means the responsibility to understand our role and the role of others in the company and to seek clarity when it is not apparent. And it is the right to be informed of the true situation with respect to our company and jobs.

Our value of equity means that we strive to achieve an equitable return for our customers, employee-owners and investors. For participative owners, this means we must work with justice and a sense of fairness. It also means we have the opportunity to share in the results (whether positive or negative) of our work. We expect the sharing to result in both financial rewards and psychic rewards.

A third value related to ownership is spirit. We value excitement, enthusiasm and energy at Herman Miller and expect people to have a positive attitude. We believe in the importance of celebration and tradition. For employee-owners, this means we share commitments to the company, its goals and to each other.

Our Herman Miller values can be summarized in just six words: innovation and excellence through participative ownership.

Judith Ramquist
Sales Development Manager

Active participant in restructuring the Scanlon program in 1979; first director of the Scanlon Office.

For most of us on the ad hoc committee, it was a very interesting education and training time. Many people had never been involved in anything corporate. There were people who had been on the production line, maybe for a number of years, and had never done anything related to Herman Miller outside their own department. Some people were fairly new to the company. Some others had worked in office positions, maybe in just one particular department with one realm of responsibility that had never put them in touch with anybody else in the company. So they were somewhat isolated.

All of a sudden, you are working with people on the committee from all around the United States—at Irvine or in the field sales organization. Or maybe you were in Accounting and you were working on a committee with a guy from the Dimension Mill. I mean you really began learning about this organization. And if you brought to the committee only your point of view from your particular area, you very quickly learned that that wasn't enough, because everybody else was talking about the way certain things you were discussing would affect them in their jobs, in their departments, in their divisions. So you learned, in spite of yourself, what went on in the various parts of the organization.

As a committee, we said, "You don't choose whether we'll stay with the old Scanlon Plan or go with the new. The old plan is no longer effective for us, and we're not going to have it anymore. So we can choose to start with the new plan, or we just won't have one."

It was a tough vote for people, because it was very complicated to figure out how we were going to suddenly begin this measurement throughout the whole company, when we had never done that before. What we had been doing, which had been very simple and easy to understand, was no longer appropriate. And that was a very hard thing, especially for people in the plant who had grown up with the Scanlon Plan, who understood it thoroughly, and who all of a sudden were having to give up something.

You began to feel out of control. "Oh, my goodness," you know. "Now everybody!" And, in addition, the field sales people were going to be included in the pay-out. That was a very hard thing to help people understand. They knew field sales people got salaries, and they also knew that they had an incentive bonus if they reached their goals. Many people said, "Why should they get more on top of that?" And, of course, the answer had to be, "Where would we be as an organization if the field sales people weren't out there bringing in the business? And *how can we measure everybody else in the company and not measure them? And if they're measured and their contribution is actually a very big one, how can we not share in the results of that measurement?''*

So it was a long series of explanations, really having conversations back and forth in groups, to help people understand that we are all in this together, or we are not all in this together.

There were some of us who felt that we should present the new plan in a very neutral way and say, "Okay, here it is. Now everybody is free to make up their minds as they see fit"—and that we wouldn't have a role as a committee in influencing them. This became a big controversy on the committee. There were several of us—and I was one—who were slow to come around to feeling we had a role as advocates.

Dr. Frost and Bill Greenwood were very helpful. They said, "Look, this is something that you people have designed. You have your heart in it and you believe in it. Now do you really feel that your job stops there? Or do you feel that you must go out as an advocate and support it and help other people to understand it?"

Even those of us who had wondered if that was our role changed. And by the end, we were strongly lobbying. Everyone on the committee had a secret ballot. I remember that most of us marked our ballot affirmatively and then stuck it up on our tackboard surface so everybody could see that we had already voted for it. So it was a really exciting time.

Dr. Carl Frost
Partner, Frost, Greenwood and Associates;
Professor Emeritus, Michigan State University

Developer of the Scanlon Plan; questioner, listener and friend; made a great difference to so many people.

When we began the program, we were on piece rates, individual piece rates; and as is typical of a company, they were somewhat erratic. For example, the person who earned the most money at Herman Miller was the person who was tying the springs underneath the sofa. At that time, the springs had to be all tied by hand, and he was awfully good at it. So he got a fabulous rate.

PEOPLE AS BEARERS OF RESPONSIBILITY

Well, in going to a program where there were no piece rates, because they were contradictory to the group plan, we had to look at what had been the earnings. So we went through the previous year, year and a half, to see what people had been earning over that period of time—to see what the variance was. If there was a great variance, a period of illness might be the explanation for it.

After we got all through and we had lined up the earnings by employee, Duke Gebben and I thought, well, shall we group them in deciles, those between ninety and one hundred, eighty and so forth?

Then D.J. came in and we gave him the set of data. D.J. said, "Well, now, what would be the honest thing to do?"

"Well," we said, "pay each one what he earned individually."

"O.K., that's what we'll do." But then he asked, "What about all of the accumulated chits?"

You see, the employees always kept some uncashed chits in cigar boxes for that rainy day when they didn't feel very good; and they might say, "Well, it's been a lousy week, but I gotta pay the rent and I gotta put this down payment on something" and so forth. D.J. wanted to know what we were going to do with those chits.

"Well," he said, "we have to be honest. What's the honest thing to do?"

And I said, "I think the honest thing to do is put them on their honor."

So we had what we called Honor Day, when they could bring all the chit boxes' contents, or they could bring some, or they could bring none. And that's exactly what they did. What was the honest thing to do was also the right thing to do.

Craig Schrotenboer
Director, Zeeland Production

Grew up with Herman Miller; understands the Scanlon process and knows how to manage through it.

We had a major crisis shortly after I started at the Holland chair plant. We found that the fabric was delaminating from our Ergon chairs. It was bubbling up, leaving the contour of the seat.

This meant that we had to go back to four different warehouses and uncarton and inspect 10,000 chairs—while still getting our normal production out. If we found chairs to be defective, we had to take them apart, we had to sew new covers, reapply the covers, and then reassemble the chairs.

How do you put your arms around that kind of a problem? What we did was to go to the organization. We went back to the first-line supervisor, and we went to the people on the floor. We asked, "How can we do this?" We said, "We need your ideas."

They came back with some marvelous solutions to what seemed to be a monumental task. They organized themselves. They knew the business. They took charge, and we went through 10,000 chairs in three days and made all the corrections while still maintaining full production.

First shift was doing regular production. Second shift would then handle all the logistics of getting the chairs from the warehouse, tearing the boxes apart, tearing the chairs apart. It was kind of like a social circle. Here we were, adults of all levels sitting in a circle of twenty-five chairs with little icepicks, all popping staples.

We did not lose any chairs, we maintained ninety-seven percent completions, and what the organization felt would be a two-week task was accomplished in three and a half days. That's because we encouraged the people who were going to be impacted by this activity to offer solutions and become involved in the work itself. And I'm convinced that the results they came up with far exceeded anything I or my staff would have been able to work out alone.

Steve Frykholm

I would like to believe I manage with participation, but I personally have a difficult time with the formal structure of Scanlon, the suggestion forms, the work teams, the caucuses. I understand it—but. Maybe it's because our group is smaller. I remember getting many PSAs [problem, suggestion, action] about why don't we change the trucks and put a slogan on them. Maybe pictures of our products—something to communicate the nature of our business. At one point Mary Sullivan and I went so far as to prototype a truck. We applied the slogan that was on our stationery at that time. I just didn't like it.

PEOPLE AS BEARERS OF RESPONSIBILITY

We rejected the idea, but it seems like nobody keeps these responses in the computer. So when business is very competitive, as it has been recently, we keep getting this idea over and over. The people in the organization, bless them, are really looking for opportunities to help communicate what we do, what we make. So this suggestion about the trucks keeps coming forth.

While I was talking with Max one day I said, "You know, about these suggestions for slogans on the trucks I keep getting—I wish I could just tell these people to buzz off."

Max said, "Why don't you?"

I said, "I can't do that."

He said, "Why not?"

I think my response was, "Well, maybe I'm just too tired to look at it again, okay?" So you sort of say, "Well, the idea is maybe okay, maybe not okay. But sometimes I wish they'd just do their jobs, and let me do mine. And trust each other. Maybe more trust would help."

Emerson in his essay "Self-Reliance" writes, "An institution is the lengthened shadow of one man." He cites as proof Luther's leadership of the Reformation, Wesley's founding of Methodism and Clarkson's leadership in the abolition movement. It was also true of Henry Ford and the Ford Motor Company and many others. Herman Miller once was the lengthened shadow of D.J. De Pree, and his beliefs continue to permeate the company. They are a foundation on which we have built.

However, Emerson continues: "Kingdom and Lordship, power and estate are a gaudier vocabulary than private John and Edward in a small house and common day's work; but the things of life are the same to both; the sum total of both is the same."

Lengthened shadows of a few giants have made and should continue to make a difference at Herman Miller. But the difference we strive for relies, too, on "private John and Edward" and the bear catchers who make things work.

All these bearers of responsibility have not only the rights we have discussed, but they also have the right to demand management and leadership who believe in the vision and values that are Herman Miller; who have the skill and will to perform and the understanding that they have no prerogatives but responsibilities. They are the leaders, the giant carriers, and I pay them tribute for their extraordinary achievements during my years of association with them.

Max De Pree organized marketing and sales in the late 1950s. He became executive vice-president and then gave that up to move with his family to Basel for one year to reorganize and lead our efforts in Europe. He returned to assume responsibility for the company's facility program as we grew so rapidly, and to chair and develop a board of directors that could meet the drastic changes in our business. He became chief executive officer when I retired.

Vernon Poest, who left the security of a family business for indistinct opportunities at Herman Miller, studied controls and finance, kept us out of bankruptcy through his intervention with the banks, taught us how to make a profit, became our executive vice-president and chief operating officer; and then, when the need arose, accepted the role of chief financial officer and led the program to "take us public."

Glenn Walters began as a salesman, became responsible for marketing a major new George Nelson program, moved to Herman Miller Research as the manager, directed all sales and marketing for Herman Miller, and became chief operating officer for U.S. Operations. His most influential and lasting role was bringing Action Office to the market. He made the most important contribution of any of us to the success of that program, moving to become, first our chief operating officer, then president when I retired.

Steve Snoey began as a bookkeeper, became the company controller with major responsibility in finance. He agreed to move to Bath, England, with his family, to take over our European operations and become chief operating officer for International.

These men knew who they were. They understood our principles, taught others, took risks, carried giants, knew people, were committed to the Scanlon Plan as the way of managing, and they built the company.

T*here are two classes of creatures: those who make great demands on themselves, piling up difficulties and duties, and those who demand nothing special of themselves, but for whom to live is to be every moment what they already are, without imposing on themselves any effort toward perfection, mere buoys that float on the waves.*

—Ortega y Gassett

Those who make great demands on themselves, who make an investment of themselves in their work, know they can make a difference. And they can convince others that their efforts, too, can make a difference. Such self-awareness is the beginning of leadership. It goes beyond management, which is a skill that can be learned from almost as many books on the subject as there are seashells on the shore. So what you will find here is not another essay on management but a personal view of leadership and the behavior demanded of leaders.

Many confuse leadership with management. They are not the same thing. Leadership provides direction, vision, philosophy, opportunity, guidance—and it works from the top down through the organization. Management, by contrast, provides plans, action, evaluation, correction, results—and because these responsibilities are best handled by those directly involved, management works from the bottom up.

Leaders and the culture of the organization develop together. They do so by mandate. The philosophy, direction, goals and design of the company, as well as the reality of the marketplace and the resources available, dictate the mandate which leadership serves. The mandate prescribes the kind of leadership needed.

Leadership, in the person of the chief executive officer, is responsible for the mandate. Defining it is one of his most important tasks. The CEO is simply not being responsible to the organization if he fails to define the direction, state the commitment, and delegate action to competent people.

At Herman Miller, we learned that without a mandate, the organization could not make the best use of the Scanlon Plan. The climate for the complete review and redesign of the Herman Miller plan, Scanlon '79, was set when our mandate was clearly defined in 1977. The mandate became clear and was issued only after much persuasion by Carl Frost and extensive work by top management. To this mandate, each leader dedicates understanding, acceptance and commitment; and the leaders promise each other and everyone connected with the business that this way of life together will be maintained and nurtured. For without that promise, leadership cannot function. In short, the mandate is the statement to which everyone in the company is subordinate. This was the Herman Miller mandate issued in 1977:

Herman Miller must be an international organization in which people define and solve problems. Problem definition and problem solving—through innovation wherever possible—must result in products and services which improve the quality of life in the working and healing environments. At Herman Miller, people have the responsibility and opportunity to contribute, to participate, to be involved, to own the problem—and, indeed, to own Herman Miller.

We are committed to quality and excellence in all that we do and the way in which we do it.

We seek to be socially responsible and we share a concern and responsibility for the quality of the environment in which we and our neighbors live and work.

LEADERSHIP: THE BELIEVERS AND DOERS

Profit is an essential and enabling factor in all annual and long range planning and operations. Specific profit goals will be set annually. Growth is implicit but must come because of the quality of the problem solution and the potential in our people and our program.

The mandate dictates the kind of leadership a business needs, but leadership can be defined even more clearly with a clear definition of the business. Clarity of meaning, however, can have its own ironic overtones. Senior vice president Bill Simmons has observed, ''Sometimes we feel disadvantaged by our mandate, but it has challenged our senior management team to confront reality. Sometimes we have to get kicked in the seat of the pants to deal with reality.''

We say that Herman Miller is a problem-solving, risk-taking, committed-to-change, dedicated-to-quality, and pursuit-of-excellence company, in which an open climate of freedom is fostered, in which people have the right and responsibility to contribute, to be involved, to influence. We do not have on blinders which commit us only to the office furniture or health care furniture business. We are open to offering products and services wherever there is work going on. This dictates the need for leaders who are willing to work through others and see that they get the credit, who are open to new ideas and have the courage to push them through, and who are then ready to be judged on the results.

A leader must accept the fact that within the organization there exist greater competence, knowledge, and skill at implementing projects he assigns than the leader alone could ever have.

There is an old story of two hunters who had hunted together for many years. They devoted much energy to trying to find a better dog. Finally, one found a superb dog, the best he had ever seen. He could hardly wait to go duck hunting, and so one morning the two hunters made their way to the duck blind. Before long, a duck was shot and the new dog's owner proudly motioned the dog out. The dog jumped out and ran across the water, picked up the duck and ran right back across the water. The second hunter was astonished. He could not believe what he saw, so he decided to say nothing. Another duck was shot, and the dog ran across the water again. Again, the second hunter said nothing. Finally, to provoke some response, the dog's owner said, "Quite a dog, isn't he? Have you noticed anything unusual about him?" His companion thought for a minute, then said, "Yep. Can't swim, can he?"

Myth: The leader is God, walks on water, and sits alone on a throne.
In truth, the leader often is not even sure he can swim. So, without yielding accountability for decisions, he evaluates his strengths and weaknesses and surrounds himself with other leaders who offset his weaknesses. It takes a team. Strength is found in diversity at the leadership level.

Myth: Put your life in my hands, for I am the leader.
Such leaders rule through fear and do not forgive failure. In so doing, they rain all over the enthusiasm of those who fail and on that of others, too. The result? Followers simply concentrate on not failing. They will not risk, and little will happen. *The Times* of London describes one of the dominant figures in British business as being "equipped with overweening ambition, enormous energy, and a skin thicker than rhinocerous hide." Would you like to work for him? Could he make a difference at Herman Miller?

Myth: Leadership is a static position. Once you have achieved leadership, you must lead in all programs and activities within your area of responsibility.
No, leadership is dynamic. Twenty years ago, in my capacity as chairman of the board of Hope College, I planned, together with the president, a critically needed

but drastic and potentially divisive reorganization of the board. On the day of implementation, I asked another board member, Judge Dale Stoppels, a man of recognized wisdom and integrity, to chair the meeting. With understanding and compassion, he guided us through this major change during which the board members voted themselves out of office, reelected a few, and then elected new members, who, with the holdovers, made up a much smaller and more effective board. The judge was the leader on that important day. Leadership rotates according to the situation.

Myth: A leader controls.
Those responsible for a project must control it, for otherwise they cannot function and don't have responsibility.

If the leader controls the project, it is likely that the job isn't being done as well as it should be. The leader, however, does make sure the right person is doing the job, and he does not give up accountability *as* the leader.

Myth: Leadership is simple.
Just the opposite. Leadership is complex, for it involves the total process of enabling people to do the right job and to do the job right, of being a resource to others, of managing conflict, defining problems and communicating with clarity, of achieving results, maintaining a balance between being informed and being involved, of providing the opportunity for self-discipline and auditing those factors important to the organization. You must portray consistency, so others know where you are, of evaluating performance and rewarding competence, and more and more. Leadership is not simple.

The myths of leadership should give us perspective. The following five rules have helped me keep the myths about leadership separate from reality:

1. Responsibility and accountability rest on the leader, but not power; power changes people and their relationships.

Power should be focused in those who own the company—both shareholders and those who own through their contributions to the organization and the dedication of their lives.

2. A leader must be open to ideas, talents, actions, and the influence of others.

3. A leader is a steward of one's own talents, gifts, experience and knowledge. Even more, a leader is a steward of the talents and resources placed in his care, as well as of the ideas, products and programs designed and developed by these resources.

4. A leader must have integrity—a natural trait, for it cannot be learned—a firm commitment to wholeness, completeness and fairness, dedicated to equity and justice.

5. A leader is willing to risk and will accept responsibility for it. Someone has said, "The whole idea of the presidency is having somebody in the Oval Office who can try to get above the bickering and buttonholing in the cloakroom and corridors and say, 'Enough of this. Let's just get something done for a change that will help the people.'"

Here, for good measure, are a few thoughts about leadership that may guide you as you think through your own notions of this factor so important to the survival and growth of a business.

A leader knows who he is. And he encourages, perhaps demands, that all who work with him make a similar discovery. Of President Eisenhower, it is said, "Somewhere along the way he has found out who he is, what he thinks, and why he thinks it. That is a rare thing for any man."

A leader earns leadership when followers are willing to follow. This does not mean there is a danger of the leader now becoming the follower; for to be a leader, one must have strong beliefs, a solid foundation and recognized principles. But the true leader knows himself well enough to know that the organization is people who will achieve better results when they are all moving in the same direction.

Leaders understand that people need the opportunity to assume responsibility. In particular, the leaders at Herman Miller know that those who believe in the values of the company and understand clearly what has to be done will assume the responsibility for how it is done and will be accountable for results. Such results can be extraordinary. Robert Woodruff, the builder and leader of Coca Cola said, ''There is no limit to what can be done if you don't care who gets the credit.'' Personally, my management style was to get people to do great things: to think of new ideas and how to implement them. I believe a leader serves well when the people say, after a project is completed and successful, ''We did it.''

Leaders do not threaten. They believe that other people, competent people, are as concerned with making the right decisions and taking the right actions as the leader is. At Herman Miller, people must have the opportunity to fail. Ed Simon puts it this way: ''We find that the most successful people in the company are the ones who really understand their weaknesses. They can tolerate other people's weaknesses and work with them at the top management level, understanding very clearly that the organization is always an imperfect organization—striving always to be more nearly perfect, but knowing it will always be imperfect. That's important, because without tolerance you can run into such problems as becoming a zealot— like I was at one time.''

Implicit in the idea of leadership is the concept of service, of being a resource. It is through serving that one leads. By providing the climate within which others can think, decide, act and possibly fail, the success of an enterprise is insured. To lead the people, walk behind them.

Leaders prepare for crisis, for the world is full of crises. They don't wait for crises to manage them. At a luncheon, I sat next to the president of Michigan State University. We discussed management style, and he described his as "management by crisis." He was wasting his time by waiting for the crisis and then managing.

A leader has courage, takes risks. James Burke, chairman of Johnson & Johnson, was faced twice in three years with the poisoning of one of their products, Tylenol. His courage in openly facing the press and his willingness to risk a major part of the company to avoid peril to people were exemplary. Several times since 1930, leaders at Herman Miller have risked the company, moving into modern furniture, giving freedom to innovative people, making complete changes in the distribution of our products, abandoning the residential business and moving into the office and then the work area with appropriate systems. Leaders take risks.

Leadership demands character, intellectual honesty and integrity. In a meeting with our management, Peter Drucker once said, "You can teach a manager all he needs to know about management, but if he does not have integrity, he will not succeed." A leader does not violate the integrity or the dignity of people. A leader offers people the gift of dignity. When Walter Reuther, leader of the autoworkers union died, a single line editorial in the *Detroit Free Press* read: "He gave them dignity."

A leader brings reality to the organization, knowing that the image of the company is necessary and must be communicated, but also knowing that a precise image is a goal, not reality. At Herman Miller, it is too easy to believe ourselves when we proudly talk about our company. A leader must occasionally remind others, just as David Hutt, managing director of Herman Miller Ltd., did not long ago when he said, "I guess one of the dangers that we have to guard against, particularly as senior managers, is that it is always easy to swallow your own propaganda. There are many other companies who practice disciplines and ways of doing business similar to Herman Miller's. I think we should be skeptical, we senior managers, that we have all the answers. I think we are good, but we're not unique.''

Leadership is constricted by slavish adherence to tight schedules, endless meetings and seclusion. A leader is reinforced, not by a completed calendar, but by roaming around unconventional places at unlikely times with his antenna out and quivering. A leader needs diversity to compensate for the normal limits of vision.

A leader can be flummoxed by an exaggerated concern for the competition. Watching the other fellow with an anxious sense of rivalry can provoke you to make decisions and do things that may harm the company. D.J. would occasionally chide me for not knowing more about Knoll, but I was more concerned with establishing direction and holding the course. If we had been more concerned with Knoll, we could easily have competed on their grounds, designing and marketing individual pieces exclusively. Had we done that, we would not have become the different kind of company we were aiming to be—the kind of company Pep Nagelkirk, a problem solver *par excellence*, refers to when he says, ''I choose not to look at what other people are doing. We're Herman Miller, you know. We're Number One. So why look at other people? Let them copy us.''

But it is not always easy to hold the course. Following a talk I made at the International Design Congress in London in 1966, Herman Miller was panned for not keeping up with Knoll in designing new products. Designers accused us of losing our push. ''The leadership is with Knoll and others,'' they claimed. ''They are moving ahead of you.''

At that moment, we were working on Action Office, but there was little reply I could make to the criticism, for it was too early to make our announcement. Of course, the answer came loud and clear only two years later.

A leader knows that recycling and renewing are vital for both personal health and the health of the organization. Courses, schools and structured experience may be helpful, but more important, a growing leader must be a searcher: one who is seeking new experiences through which one's growth can be nurtured and expanded. Such experiences are most valuable when they are unrelated to one's own responsibilities. It takes a unique leader to engage in and lead renewal, to foster the quality of life in the organization. And in the end, when a leader retires or goes on to other challenges, he should have confronted a departing responsibility: He must have left impounded energy in the organization.

A leader confronts contradictions, deals with them, and tries to be a resolver and connector, not a deterrent. Contradictions are not just conflicting opinions and disagreements but actually a way of life: uniformity should not be expected.

The Bible says, ''The greatest of these is love.'' But in churches since the days of the Apostles, love has often been absent in emotional confrontations about meaning or practice. People throughout the world desire peace, but nations go to war to avenge wrongs. People in the South Bronx may live in filth and decay, while, nearby, others worry about tax deductions for interest on palatial second or third homes.

Businesses succeed or fail with different strategies and goals; some, like the acquisition hunters with their junk bond financing, are dedicated only to making money. Others recognize the need for profit but are just as dedicated to serving society. At Herman Miller we have seen contradictions between every man for himself and helping each other through participation, profits today and investment in the future, design and research. In our first meeting with Peter Drucker, he defined a contradiction: Our annual sales were thirty million dollars, but our program was designed to be effective at seventy million.

LEADERSHIP: THE BELIEVERS AND DOERS

A leader knows there will be contradictions and, to understand them, often must see things from the perspectives of other people, the different ways those offering advice and information see the situation and the solution. The leader must decide the truth in terms of the direction that has been defined. The leader must ask, ''What is good for this business?'' I believe confronting contradictions and the sifting of them is one of the more difficult but important responsibilities of the leader.

Courage, integrity, humility, service—these are the hallmarks of leadership and these characteristics must be at the core of Herman Miller or any other business as business can be. But there is a cost for being this kind of leader. You have to continue the learning process as long as you live. Credit, recognition and honor—these belong to those who, although working with you, have been directly involved and have earned them.

Finally, here are some questions a leader should ask.

What difference are you making in this organization?

What can I do to help you? What do you need from me?

What are you doing to help me do my job better?

Do you understand the mandate? Do you know our objectives?

What don't you understand?

Do you know who you are and how you affect others? What are your strengths and weaknesses—and what are you doing about them? What have you done lately to rock the boat?

Do you feel you can influence anything here?

Do you own this place?

Several years ago, sitting in a room over the Miami River, I was preparing a talk for the annual sales meeting.

It was my last opportunity to speak to this group. I wanted to speak to them about the important things at Herman Miller: the need for connections in our relationships and the continuing need for a quality of leadership that would carry us forward in the decade to come. Pondering these thoughts, I noticed out the window a cargo ship being towed up the river to a berth. It looked like a normal tow until I spotted something special going on astern. A smaller tug whose name I made out to be the *Maya* had a line to the stern of the cargo vessel. The *Maya*, with this line taut, dashed back and forth making sure the ship stayed headed in the right direction.

A picture of Herman Miller became clear. Obviously by now, most of the crew knew where they were going and what they were to do when they arrived. The lead tug was supplying the ''go,'' the power that was needed. To me, this was a metaphor for the hundreds of people involved in and contributing to Herman Miller. The *Maya* was a symbol of my role as a leader, the person who had to know where the organization was going, and that getting there wasn't a one-man task. The entire scene was a picture of a team.

One person can't lead or perpetuate an organization. It takes a team. For the team is the new genius of our time.

There is a pattern in the affairs of a company. The principles and beliefs, encounters and events, people and performance—all continually design and redesign the business. At Herman Miller, part of this pattern is the series of crises and fortuitous encounters that have played a major role in the design of this company. Crisis in business is not unusual, and neither are the subsequent events that may radically affect the organization. We see this happening almost daily in an age when extreme competition and uncertainty lead to acquisitions and mergers and tremendous change in companies and industries.

An aspect of Herman Miller is that the crises which changed the company were the results of self-examination and were based on the principles which have guided this company since its early days. These crises were, first, the definition of the problems in the furniture industry; second, the sudden death of Gilbert Rohde; third, the vision that each person is extraordinary and can contribute to the business; fourth, the change from representation in the market to an integrated sales and marketing program; and fifth, the rapid move from residential furniture to systems and furniture for work in the office, factory and health care facilities.

Each of these crises was solved through a fortuitous encounter with a giant. First, with Gilbert Rohde, who showed us a new way of living in the home; second, with George Nelson, who revised our thinking about our world and became part of management; third, with Carl Frost, who brought reality and change to our life and work at Herman Miller; fourth, we discovered we had excellent talent within the company, with Max De Pree organizing a radical change in sales and marketing and then with Glenn Walters building on that; and fifth, with Robert Propst, whose ideas about how people should work forced the most radical change in this company's history.

Could dependence only on education and training enable anyone to resolve such crises? Could reliance only on scientific management enable one to sense the benefits of a relationship with George Nelson, Charles Eames or Robert Propst? It's doubtful.

Fortuitous encounters, which solve crises, happen because principles are clear and those responsible for solving problems are roaming widely through society, seeing and thinking about things visible and invisible. These events have also been described as providential. It may be, however, that God doesn't directly lead or guide us to solutions but rather that there is a connection between deep faith and the willingness to confront, believing that if we are willing to listen, to be open, to trust and to risk, a solution will appear.

The principles are basic. They generate the deep roots on which the company is designed, the enterprise to which so many are committed and in which they choose ownership. These roots give us shared values which blossom through the events and relationships we have discussed in this book.

A reprise is played in operas and musicals, distilling for us the important messages we have heard. So, too, can our understanding of the past distill the important principles which give us definition and life.

VISION AND VALUES

Vision is the ability to perceive something that is not actually visible or apparent. It is an imaginative force that influences and changes our lives. In the world we know, vision has changed society, industry and our lives.

Gandhi had a vision of an independent Indian nation governed by a free people ruling their own destiny and claiming their place in the world.

REPRISE

Martin Luther King had vision: "a dream that one day this nation will rise up and live out the true meaning of its creed, 'We hold these truths to be self-evident—that all men are created equal.'"

Woodrow Wilson had a vision, that all nations could join together to outlaw war, and he helped form The League of Nations.

Franklin Roosevelt had a vision of government providing a more equal society, influencing and changing our lives.

D.J. De Pree had a vision that a business should be "rightly judged by its humanity," and that everyone should have the right to identity, equity and opportunity. He also had a vision of a company that would bring in designers who would study the problems of living, linked in their pursuit with a manufacturer who would trust them to provide appropriate solutions.

George Nelson had a vision of Herman Miller—a company that would have a cheerful indifference to what the rest of the industry might be up to. He believed that what you make is important and that design is an integral part of the business.

Carl Frost had a vision that the division of labor and management could be unified to enable everyone to have the opportunity to participate and to be an involved part of the business.

Robert Propst had a vision of the way the office, the factory and health-care activities should work, and of how people could work and live in such facilities.

I had a vision that Bob Propst's concepts could improve the quality of life in the office and that these ideas could be brought to the market in innovative ways. These visions combined to change the world of work in the office.

We had a vision of a business dedicated to solving problems in the living, learning, working and healing environments.

Max De Pree had a vision that those who devoted their

lives to, and were involved in, the business should not only own it through their ideas, contributions and influence, but should also be participating shareholders in it.

Without vision we are living only for today. With vision we are not only ready for change, we are making it. But vision does not come with a flash of light and a roll of thunder. The foresight which enables one to see what is not normally apparent begins with "local knowledge," the understanding of who we are, and the reality of our resources. Thus prepared, one may be able to define the problem and then begin viewing it in many and different ways. George Nelson's book *How to See* offers superb thinking for such an expanded perception.

Vision is part of the creative process. It is not restricted to any elite group, for we know that it can and does permeate an entire visionary company. Vision at Herman Miller has resulted in leading, forcing and selling change that makes work and health-care places more effective and provides a setting wherein more of the joy of life in such facilities may be realized.

Often, a visionary company seizes the initiative in defining and solving problems, not only for its own benefit, but for society's as well. At Herman Miller such initiative has frequently seemed an appropriate way to add our contribution to society while realizing the goals of mutual advantage through a variety of relationships. What we have attempted in the education field illustrates this kind of contribution.

At Clear Creek School in Idaho Springs, Colorado, we collaborated some years ago with the nonprofit Educational Facilities Laboratory and Clear Creek's superintendent, Robert Metzler, in a problem-solving adventure.

Together, we studied problems associated with both the physical structure—the school buildings—and also the "feeling" of the school, the way it conveys respect or lack of it and thus how it affects learning within the facility. New values in the school environment were proposed, an actual physical environment was designed, and suggestions for implementation were outlined. These solutions were offered to educators in a book published by EFL and Herman Miller.

In New York City's Harlem, the Herman Miller Research Corporation once made substantial investments of resources and talent in a street academy for the disadvantaged. Here, in a renovated supermarket building adapted for school use by a portable interior furnishing system, the students were graduated only after being accepted by a college. The problems of the physical facility and the learning climate were defined and solved through the joint efforts of Herman Miller Research and Ed and Ann Carpenter, who founded and operated Harlem Prep. Helping to create a learning environment in an ex-supermarket seemed an appropriate response to a community need.

Similarly, our research corporation joined EFL and the University of Massachusetts during the height of the student protest era to examine the influence of the living environment on the attitudes and behavior of students in high-rise dormitories. We regarded this project as a stern test for the wide-ranging social and environmental research inquiries being generated at that time by Bob Propst and his associates in Ann Arbor.

The first step at the University's Amherst campus was to define the problem. The high-rise dormitories were not happy places. The students complained about the dirt, the isolation in a cell-like existence, and it was hardly surprising that serious psychological problems had developed. Vandals conducted a mean-spirited kind of guerrilla warfare against their surroundings; a bleak, treeless, inhumanely scaled brick courtyard was dubbed Red Square by students. Lounges were ripped up, furniture stolen, drop ceilings in the elevators torn out. Keeping the lights working became a contest, and trash thrown out the window was a visual norm.

Two main problems were defined: first, the lack among

the students of any feeling of ownership; and second, a pattern of isolated and disconnected friendships rather than any coherent social context to nurture a sense of community.

Herman Miller Research proposed a test involving forty students. They would be provided with new furnishings and services that would allow them a wide range of individual options and expressions. Two floors were selected for major overhauling. Floors were carpeted. Doors and hallways were painted in colors and designs selected by the students from several alternatives. All rooms were refurnished with specially designed furniture, including a number of novel ideas such as self-making beds.

For both practical and socially strategic reasons, a resource "general store" was established on each floor. It offered additional furniture, accessories, tools, hardware and other service items. Here students could rent products they needed to make their rooms more livable, or they could rent items to help them in their studies. That was the practical side of the general store. Equally important, it was designed and intended to be the university's front-line means to listen to, talk with, trade with and serve its students.

In addition to our design and material support, Herman Miller Research contributed the on-site services of a deeply committed young woman, virtually a contemporary of the students, to make the whole program fly. She was Claudia Propst, one of the four children of Bob and Lee Propst who at one time or another worked alongside the Propsts' "extended family," which comprised the research company's work force.

The Massachusetts project produced no miraculous changes in student attitudes or behavior, but it more than met the performance objectives set by the university. The improvements were consistent and significant. Different and better ways of living in dormitories were tested, useful products and services were designed—and the project was turned over to the university.

Within a visionary company, timing is particularly important in research and development. While each of these and other projects produced new tools and insights for education, time was against their continuation. Federal funds for schools were cut, and educators returned to traditional methods and structures. They could no longer afford the risk of innovation, despite the obvious need for better solutions.

But for Herman Miller, these were, and still are, the rich rewards of a visionary outlook. We had been involved with a fundamentally important segment of society, defining and solving some of education's problems; and in so doing, we had contributed in an appropriate way to society at large.

Vision should also be part of our personal life. What is your vision of your life? What are the accomplishments you wish to achieve? What will be your contribution to society? In *Death of a Salesman*, Charley says to Willy Loman, "No man needs only a little salary." We all need salary, but we receive lasting satisfaction from the ability to dream dreams—to have vision about needs and opportunities.

The escort of vision is values. It is the values we hold that reveal our interests, our priorities, *who we are*. Not long ago I sat in a waiting room at my doctor's office. The television screen showed the astronauts walking in space and wrestling to retrieve a satellite. Almost everyone ignored this scene, preferring to read the *Miami Herald*. The program changed, and Dean Martin appeared telling what he thought of Shirley MacLaine, Frank Sinatra and Sammy Davis, Jr. The whole room perked up. The patients put away their newspapers, the nurses and the receptionist left their duties to watch the entire segment. Values were being revealed.

What are the fundamental values on which we stand at Herman Miller and which must be woven into the organization? I count the following values to be essential.

Excellence: In what we do and the way we do it.

Openness: The right and responsibility of all competent people to be appropriately informed so they can contribute.

Participation: The right and responsibility of people to participate, to influence and to contribute to our direction and performance through their ideas, decisions and work. It is in this value that we also assert the fundamental value of the person.

Ownership: The right of employees to own the business, to make it their own place as a result of their contributions, and also to help direct Herman Miller as participating shareholders.

Social responsibility: We expect to be a part of and a contributor to the communities in which we work and live.

The Scanlon Plan: It provides us with the best alternative we have for managing the business.

Products and services: What we make is important and it matters to us. We are dedicated to good design. We will make products and systems, along with appropriate services, that solve problems in working and living and add richness to life.

Environment: We have concern for the environment in which we work. The property and facilities we develop for our use must improve the quality of life in the communities we serve.

We seek people who will accept these values, for a business is not defined by the assets it shows on the balance sheet, nor by the profit it makes, nor only by the products it makes. Rather, it is defined by the beliefs and values held by its people.

Vision and values: A two-pronged force that is part of the foundation on which we build.

REPRISE

EXCELLENCE AND QUALITY

*We are committed to quality and ex-
cellence in all that we do and the way in
which we do it.*

—Herman Miller Mandate

At Chewton-Mendin near Bath, England, a cheddar cheese dairy still makes cheese the old-fashioned way—by the hands of skilled and committed people. These craftsmen carefully control the process as the materials pass through spotless tanks into long, waist-high vats in which they vigorously stir and paddle, draining off the curds until the mixture begins to become firm and turns a sunset gold color. The resultant product is ladled into copper containers of various sizes and stored for curing. This dairy offers a lesson in excellence. Quality shines in every piece of equipment. It is expressed in the workers' satisfaction as they tamp the cheese into the containers, and then as they scrub and clean up with an air of, ''We have done it well again.''

Charles Eames talked about ''good goods,'' and that is exactly what these cheesemakers were producing. The process and the product bespeak quality—cheese as good as it can be. The entire operation has an aura of excellence that made me feel on my visit there that I had spent a wonderful half day.

Why can't we live in an aura of quality? It often seems that there must be enemies conspiring to make certain things are as mediocre as they can be. What are these foes of quality? Here are a few of the more pervasive ones I've encountered.

Expediency: The self-induced need or desire to finish—to be driven, not by how well a job should be done, but by how fast.

Entropy: The degradation of an organization's commitment to the standards that have been set for quality.

Malign neglect: The purposeful erosion of quality for reasons unrelated to the product or service—perhaps to increase profit.

Forgetfulness: The human factor—''I just wasn't thinking.''

Misguided understanding of standards: The failure of management to communicate clearly.

Leveling: The fruitless notion of trying to make something acceptable for everyone. Of such people, Samuel Johnson wrote, ''Sir, your levelers wish to level down as far as themselves, but they cannot bear leveling up to themselves.''

Size: The organization has grown too big and can't afford to devote the attention it should to its products.

Whenever a company is tempted to focus on size, someone should stand up and shout or run up a storm flag. Of course, there are advantages and benefits in size. We learned from Peter Drucker that a company, like an adolescent boy, must expect that whatever fits today will be too small tomorrow. He advised us at one critical point that we needed to grow to the $70 million range to support the programs we had begun. However, size must not be a primary goal. Growth should come as a result of vision, risk, innovation, quality products and services—and energetic people. Staying on the leading edge in all these matters will produce growth and an enviable position in the industry.

We can defeat the foes of quality if we care enough about what we do. But we also need standards and goals against which we can measure what we do.

We need benchmarks of quality, as exemplified by a rosewood box I treasure—along with the story behind it.

In May, 1979, I attended my last manufacturing conference before retiring. I spoke to this group about the meaning of our company mandate, following which, to my surprise, I was given a solid gold, 18-carat Herman Miller logo. This beautiful object weighed perhaps a half pound and bore the inscription, "Excellence in Management." I will never forget the occasion or the award. But what I remember most joyfully is the box in which the gift came. It had been hand carved from solid rosewood. The top and bottom were neatly hinged and fitted together with certain precision. The rosewood finish was velvet soft, making the box marvelous to hold, to feel, even to fondle. The interior was carefully lined with a soft, deep blue fabric.

This rosewood case had been made with love and care by Herman Miller's gifted model maker, Pep Nagelkirk. Pep, in this work of his hands and mind and heart, had conveyed perfectly the whole idea of excellence. He had fully satisfied the benchmarks of quality, as elicited by questions such as these:

Does this solve the problem?

Have I injected into this the care and concern expected of me?

Is it as good as I can make it?

Is it as good as it can be?

How much of myself have I poured into this?

Do I feel good about it?

Have we built into it reliability?

Have we built into it predictability? Will this be consistent and up to expectations?

Have we built into it durability? How will it look in ten years?

Does it have value?

John Ruskin in his essay on value wrote, "It's unwise to pay too much but it's unwise to pay too little. When you pay too much you lose a little money, that is all. When you pay too little you sometimes lose everything because the thing you bought was incapable of doing the thing you bought it to do. The common law of Business Balance prohibits paying a little and getting a lot. It can't be done. If you deal with the lowest bidder it's well to add something for the risk you run. And if you do that you will have enough to pay for something better.''

There are varieties of excellence and varied definitions of it. One way to help us understand excellence is to remind ourselves of things we have seen or know of that were just right, that were as good as they can be. Here are some of my favorite things that are quintessentially right: Beethoven's Sixth Symphony; Burl Ives singing ''Cool Water''; the scene showing the hostess arranging the dinner table and then the guests at the table in the film Charles Eames did for IBM at the New York World's Fair; the ritual of presenting flowers to the soprano soloist following her aria; the change of character in actors and actresses as they quickly convert from relaxation to performance on the set of Irma La Douce; Sam Snead hitting the golf ball; Johnny Unitas directing his football team down the field; watching Armstrong's first step on the moon; Yul Brynner and Deborah Kerr moving into ''Shall We Dance?'' in the musical The King and I; the Porsche 911; the DCM chair by Eames; the pencil sharpener on the wall in second grade; the commencement address by a professor of philosophy named D. Ivan Dykstra to the Hope College class of 1976.

For each of us there are such vivid impressions to help us define excellence.

Excellence and quality cannot exist without commitment, and commitment comes through leadership: specifically, the definers and influencers of quality in the organization. Quality is a leadership responsibility, and any problem within the drive for quality is a management problem. The door is often open to the foes of quality because leadership has not demanded enough.

In this country, where quality is concerned, we're too smart for our own good. We know we can't produce goods with "zero defects," so we permit plus or minus tolerances. This may no longer be good enough. It is time that leaders should send this message throughout the organization: "We must have no defects. Anytime you see something wrong, you must pull the plug and stop the line." For it is leaders who must state the philosophy and set the direction of the company. If the leader states, as the Chairman of U.S. Steel did, that "our business is making profit," then the entire song of the business is sung to that refrain, and the individuals in the business will interpret it to mean, "My goal is to make more money for me here."

Leaders lead to excellence through these six C's: commitment, competence, care, consistency, communication and checking.

Follow-up, inspection and checking are necessary, for they serve as reminders of the agreed-upon goals for quality. Many years ago at Herman Miller, we decided we needed "principal inspecting." No piece could be shipped unless my father, D.J., my brother Max or I had inspected and initialed it. It helped make each worker to feel more responsible about the work. They became more involved because they knew that D.J., Max and I cared about each piece. It is still necessary in our company for the CEO and other top managers periodically to devote major time and attention to specific quality problems. This, too, is part of communication.

Excellence is not the exclusive realm of an elite group. Managing the business through the Scanlon Plan extends the principle of excellence to every activity of the company and fosters it through every degree of ability. It becomes the goal of everyone to help elevate the level of quality and, through this pursuit, to improve their quality of life as well as that of those who use the company's products and services. From the beginning of the Scanlon Plan, some feared its rewards for improved productivity would encourage the participants to find short cuts or produce questionable goods—a form of malign neglect. However, the plan is designed to accommodate that problem, since defective pieces and mistakes are deducted under the formulas used. Moreover, we found that workers who also understand that they are owners accept quality responsibility, because they want to produce good goods.

As a company grows, there is danger of losing this family commitment to excellence. It is management's role—through communication, example, training and orientation—to make sure that everyone understands, accepts and is committed to the standards set. At all levels of the organization, you must accept responsibility for your quality.

Not everyone attracted to a business by its philosophy, direction and standards is ready to contribute to the goals of quality. It is management's job to provide the opportunity for learning, and this may best be done by teaching. My understanding of excellence expanded remarkably one night in Los Angeles while in Charles Eames' company. It was 1954, and Charles and I had been working together at his office. Toward day's end, Charles said, "Tonight we are working on a film at home. Come along and help. We'll begin about ten o'clock." That was late for me, raised as I was where the sidewalks were rolled up at nine.

When I arrived, Charles and his film director friend Billy Wilder had just begun. Charles was experimenting with a film on toys. I will never forget the experience. The setting was a backdrop of white paper. Little pieces of mesquite were bushes. For two or three hours we wound up little toys, running them through these tiny make-believe bushes and trees; because Charles wanted to know which way they were likely to go.

Finally, Charles was ready to run some film. Billy Wilder had a car and a motorcycle. I had a car and a bird. The cars had to be run through exactly right, and I had to swoop the bird through the scene at just the right time and place, so that my fingers didn't show on the film. We did that until three or four in the morning. By that time Charles had shot no more than fifty feet of film. It was an exhausting experience—exhausting but exhilarating.

I learned that night that it was important to care, it was important to be concerned about what you were doing, that the details were vital. I learned about quality. I learned about excellence. I discovered that I could continually learn such lessons, particularly from Charles, for the rest of my life. Not least of these lessons is that, in a group, teaching is the responsibility of the leaders. Learning is an individual responsibility and it's up to you. You must accept responsibility for your own quality.

The key to quality is in the standards we set and by which we are judged. The goal of quality is reached only in our striving for excellence. Standards, goals and the intensity of our pursuit define unchanging requirements which must be continually rediscovered.

A restaurant in Illhaeusern, Alsace—L'auberge de I'll Freres Haeberlin—is owned by two brothers. One is a chef and the other an artist. Together they have discovered the harmony between food and place and the celebration of dining. Every detail whispers affirmation of quality and excellence. This place is 270 miles from Paris, but people make the drive for luncheon or dinner. Reservations must be made four to six weeks ahead. To those who might say it's not worth it, a conclusive rejoinder would be that for twenty years every table has been reserved for luncheon and dinner.

It is in the pursuit of quality that our future lies, not merely in the battle for increased market share or net income.

INNOVATION AND RISK

The rate at which energy is generated inside the sun corresponds to the explosion of a trillion one-megaton hydrogen bombs every one billionth of a second.

The Hubble space telescope will allow observation of objects near the edge of the universe, fourteen billion light years away. It will orbit the earth at an altitude of 320 miles, collecting light with electronic sensors so sensitive they could detect a flashlight beam directed at earth from the moon.

Composites made with a resin base have been around for a while, but metal matrix is something new. It's more difficult, because you must put the silicon carbide into the metal while it is in a molten state. You get a super strong material at a minimum weight.

The space program, despite its accidents, may well be the ultimate in innovation today. Years ago, Pioneer 10 left earth and it has now departed our solar system, becoming the first man-made spacecraft that has journeyed beyond our planets. Scientists chartered Pioneer's course for the next 800,000 years and calculate that its first encounter with a star will occur in 10,507 years. Thus far, only two instruments aboard have failed. A magnatachometer burned out and a star sensor was damaged when it crossed Jupiter's giant belts of radiation on December 4, 1973.

At these levels of space exploration, it is difficult for most of us to think about innovation. The innovations in space and, of course, in the military, where we have been the most effective with innovation, are mind boggling. But we need only to look around us at most businesses to restore our perspective. For we find, not innovation but Tories who want nothing to happen for the first time. Or we see gatekeepers who once found a niche and now spend all their resources protecting it for themselves and their families.

We know the stylists who offer cosmetic changes which they loudly proclaim as innovations. At the very bottom are the followers, those companies without any ideas of their own who copy those who risk innovation; those usurpers who live every moment for what's next while at the same time shouting to the public, "We are problem solvers!"

Innovation is more than "introducing something new." And it is not merely something that happens. Innovation is done by innovators, so the first secret is to find people who dare, who risk, who listen to others and are open to their ideas, who approach a problem with self-abandonment and figure out how to reach a solution. Bob Propst talks about "innovation phenomenon" and proposes that nobody is born with innovative skills or abilities; rather he feels that they creep up on the individual through lifetime experiences and events. And once they are securely in mind, the innovator can use these experiences and events to function in the frontier areas where really different things are tried and where radical solutions are possible.

But an innovator must encounter those who are willing to try drastic changes with their lives and provide the leverage and resources needed. The innovator counters with an appropriate sense of responsibility and discipline to fit these resources. Innovation begins with the definition of a problem, and the knowledge of resources and materials that may be useful in working toward a solution. The ability to look at these resources in a different way, to make connections, to let chance occur and understand when to move in—it all becomes part of the process. Innovation requires an acceptance of contradiction, and the innovator needs pertinacity to overcome the organization which is largely made up of people who, having a regular job to do, rebel at an experiment because they cannot accept the risk.

I believe that finding innovators is not likely to occur as the result of careful planning. It will more likely come from fortuitious encounters. Courting such encounters is the responsibility of leadership, for it is leaders who must be roving widely through society, meeting large and diverse numbers of people. (I refer you to the essay on leadership for fuller comment.) Our experience at Herman Miller confirms the concept of fortuitous encounters. Each of the giants who forced and enabled design and redesign of the company joined us as a result of a fortuitous encounter.

Fortuitous encounter is also part of the innovation and design process. During the development of the plastic chair, Charles Eames came to a dead stop because he was ahead of the available technology. He decided to look at other materials and by chance met a manufacturer of wire baskets. Charles's curiosity led him to study this method of molding wire mesh and, seeing its promise, he designed an upholstered wire chair. While he worked with wire mesh, fiberglass technology caught up to his original ideas, whereupon he picked up where he had left off and finished the plastic chair design.

In 1960, Robert Propst lay in the University Hospital in Ann Arbor with a severe back problem. Observing the hospital routine, he thought through many unmet needs for patient care. A critical problem he identified was the difficulty of cleaning and maintaining hospital furnishings. He designed CoStruc, a system of molded plastic units, but such components could not be made at that time. With patience stretched thin, Propst and his associates and we in management worked with resource after resource until technology and materials finally caught up with his designs. The system went to market almost ten years after its conception.

But none of this happens in any organization unless there is a climate for innovation. That can only be established through the mandate, the philosophy and the clear definition of innovation as a goal for the business.

Charles Eames believed we placed too much emphasis on innovation and argued that it was dangerous to try to be first or to be unique. He felt it required too much attention, leaving too little to making things better. But he also gave us a valuable perspective of this aspiration when he said, ''Hugh, the reason I am so frustrated with your drive for innovation is that true innovation is a function of a series of unexpected things coming together at a point in time.'' As an example, he used the French Revolution's seemingly unrelated but inexorable social and political causes. He was telling us that without these external dynamics, nothing will happen, that you can't program major change. He added, ''The only thing I can do is to try to help you recognize it when it happens, and then take advantage of it.''

I believe innovation is a way of life and it must permeate the entire company. Such a way of life cannot be turned on and off, for it is part of the nature of the business; and if it isn't, the identity changes and a different path will be followed. This way of life is the responsibility of senior management, since innovators may be mavericks who thrive on the freedom of being outside. Innovators may have little use for what has been done before, and management must become a champion for them. Since innovation is by nature so threatening to an organization, leaders who champion innovation may have to live with a high degree of self-abandonment and risk.

Innovation and risk are connected. There will be no innovation without risk, and the more difficult or the larger the problem, the more risk must be accepted, if only because the solutions may be more complex. The effect of innovation on the business defines the size of the risk. Normally, to cure what ails us, we can reorganize, hire people, borrow money, merge companies, usually with confidence, because we can marshal the vital information which clearly guides to a decision. But a few times in the life of a business, an innovation demands change and commitment that cannot be measured by information, committees or normal standards. It is then that the decision maker must risk and gamble his future and perhaps that of the company. It is the opportunity, the ability and willingness to do this that ultimately makes the difference.

To be truly innovative, to change the world a little, management sets the course, weighs the potential gain or loss and sees the change through. A company that innovates—which is to say, brings new ideas, products and systems to society and thereby establishes itself as a leader and assumes the burden of maintaining that leadership—must accept risk as a basic element of business.

IMAGE AND REALITY

We live in an age of image making. We are flooded to near suffocation with media messages designed to convince us something is better than, or different from, what it really is. And like drug addicts, we tend to live in a euphoria which requires that we convince ourselves—or become resigned to feeling—that it doesn't matter. More and more, it is becoming difficult to distinguish between appearance and reality, event and non-event, portrait and sitter, original and copy.

The tidings in this book—the reality, if you will—are that there can be a different way to build a business. This reality can be blurred by image making, as we have all discovered for ourselves.

Spend an hour in a large department store, as I did not long ago in Miami, trying to see the company—to determine what kind of people run the place. I got a confused image. The only unifying design was a sea of chrome-plated racks which were apparently thought suitable to display anything from dresses to pots and pans. To show ladies' wear, these racks often were topped with cheap little cardboard signs bearing such designer names as Lanz, Sasson or Dior. The display's image was wholly at odds with the ideas and quality of these designers. Everywhere, there were hopeless attempts at architectural variety. Attempts at visual excitement were evident in the form of gold strands dangling from ceilings; they were no more exciting than processed cheese on white store bread.

Similar sightseeing tours of stores in other cities will reveal a surprising sameness. One wonders, am I in Saks or Filenes Basement? Apparently, merchandising has become so contrived, so stereotyped, that is has obliterated any relationship between the store and what its owners stand for. Image is created by set designers who occasionally apply the cosmetics of marble and mirrors to fool us into believing we are in the midst of quality.

The marketing group for a manufacturer proposes an advertising and public-relations program that seeks to tell people, here is a company that cares—that produces quality and gives the best service in the industry. Ask the question, "What is the data for this program?" What is the response? A blank stare. Data is unimportant.

The *London Sunday Mirror* promotes its own bingo games, offering one million pounds, to increase circulation. Five pages are devoted to pushing the game. Circulation goes up, then falls after the game is over. In the meantime, the paper's owners hope advertisers will believe the *Mirror* really has increased its readership.

The image of a quiet, genteel, aristocratic eighteenth-century life in Rossborough Manor in Ireland is jarred in a marvelous, exquisitely furnished living room by very recent family pictures taken in the 1980s.

A designer's recently completed office and workshop portrays a distorted image: It is a clinically clean showroom. But give it time. Two months of working on it, strewing drawings around, accumulating sawdust and oil on the floor, and it will be a near perfect image of what such a shop really should be.

A showroom entrance is equipped with trim, little traditional windows looking out to nowhere but hung with curtains. Such a setting, for a company committed to innovation and systems, suggests a confused intention and blurs the image for everyone.

A small company manufacturing window screen has named itself EST—Environmental Screen Technology.

Daniel Boorstin in *The Image* discusses pseudo-events and a new kind of celebrity whose claim to fame is the fame itself. Far from being heroes, they are well known for the high degree of notoriety they have earned. Today we have prime-time sports programs called "Battle of the Stars" and a new low "Sports Battles of the Network Stars." Today's heroes are rock singers, film stars and athletes who make millions playing games. Politicians have learned the publicity game and aim for celebrity status. Even businessmen are catching the fever. CEOs, headlined as celebrities, begin to admire their own image and expect to be idolized by their employees and friends. Among businessmen particularly, I think competence should still be the test, with recognition coming in its own good time.

Image making is the magician's art, creating an illusion so that we mistake the image for reality. Images blot out ideals and it is shockingly easy to lose sight of ideals, but when that happens, business itself will change.

Dr. Carl Frost—on whom we at Herman Miller have leaned in times of crises, or major decision making, and when we needed common sense—has a favorite question: "What day is it?" It is a question he has used in clinical psychology to determine the patient's degree of reality. It is also useful beyond the clinic, for it is reality we must honestly work with. It should be reality that provides the driving force in our behavior.

Image and reality join together through a clearly defined mandate, and image is then most clearly evident in the products and services offered by the business. But in an organization, the buildings and equipment, the literature, offices, letterheads, trucks, the voice of the receptionist, the tone of a letter, the attitude of a salesman—all create an image.

Image must be based on reality, for there is no other honest way of telling who we are. Because an image is portrayed by people, it may blur occasionally. We must rely on leaders to guard against benign interpretations which may gradually change the image. A change in image may change the company, because image is communication and people respond to it. Image, when true, is an asset of the business.

When we discuss image we do need to be ready to throw a cup of cold water. We can, in all honesty, talk too much about our image, until we magnify it beyond reality. Then we are in danger of beginning to fall for our own rhetoric. We may feel we're a different company, but there are others that can make this same claim. Herman Miller is not the only company dedicated to innovation, and we do not have the exclusive right to the idea of participative management. But we do embody these values and therefore must remain committed to them. And we do want our image to be a reflection of what we do with these values, because without such commitment and an accompanying understanding of reality, our image may wash away.

I was dining one rainy night in a roadside restaurant near Dallas. A pond collected in the road outside, and in the water I saw a reflection of a U-Haul sign. Cars passed by and roughed the water. The image of the U-Haul sign would blur, then become clear again. Finally, the rain stopped and the water began to drain away. By the time I finished eating, only the U remained. A quite different image.

Building and keeping an image is not that simple, but the core of effort must be reality and the integrity of the company—and the integrity of the image.

BUSINESS AS UNUSUAL

VISION AND VALUES

Dick Ruch

A career at Herman Miller is exciting, but it is also demanding and consuming because you get so involved with the company—more so than you want to at times. Somehow or another, the value system keeps sending the message, and in not-so-subtle ways, that one ought to try to serve the company by doing what the corporation requires, as opposed to what you personally would like to do. There's a lot of pressure here because you're accountable up, down, and sideways in a Scanlon environment. But you've got other people to help you. Hugh, Max, they never ducked their responsibility if you asked for help. And you've got people from the side and from below who are also interested in helping solve a problem. And that really makes it a lot more fun, and it makes it possible to be successful here.

Robert Wood
Director, Marketing/Product Development,
Herman Miller United Kingdom

Part of the original Herman Miller group in England; clearly understands where we have come from and who we are today.

Here in Europe, and probably also in the States, we've suffered a great deal from unemployment in recent years. So I think people's whole perspective on what a job means, what work means, has altered. People are now giving a lot more care to the decision of what company they work for, where the company is located, and, inherently, the value system a company has. One of the questions people ask is, "What is this company about?" They are asking more questions than just, "How much will I be paid if I come to work for this company?"

What is Herman Miller about? It's very easy to fall into some trite reply to this question. But we talk a lot about the pursuit of excellence at Herman Miller, and the ability to achieve excellence in all that we do as one of the fundamentally important things here. People realize that they are going to have an opportunity to use their skill and their knowledge within the com-

pany. That is going to be appreciated and valued, and if they can push the boundaries out even further, then they're going to be encouraged to do so.

We always look for champions to make something happen. When we look at anything in Herman Miller's history, it's never been achieved without a champion.

The level of commitment we get is extremely high; when people go home, they feel they have been highly involved in their work. I don't know what response you've been getting from talking to people here, but I would say, and the evidence would show, that they do feel highly involved. We recently had an open house at Herman Miller. I would say that people, in the upper ninety percents, brought their families and friends to Herman Miller. We had as many here as the place could handle. Something like over 1,000 people came through the doors on the Saturday we had the place open.

It was amazing. Everybody took up the challenge. We had some fantastic self-generated demonstrations or expressions of what we did. You could sense the pride everybody felt: "This is not only where we work but where we're proud to be." You could see in all of these little exhibits how everybody felt they were contributing to the whole. To me, I came away with my family feeling this was a good place to belong.

In the end, if you can get that sort of spirit, that sort of commitment, it's difficult to see how you can't succeed. Because when you've got everybody working with you, toward the common objective, it takes a lot of stopping.

There has to be an origin and a purpose to everything, and if you look at Herman Miller as a business—putting it into a business context—the roots of what you are doing are terribly important. When we travel from England, which is a country steeped in history, when we go to the United States, we are always aware of the youthfulness of the country: the vibrance, the opportunity. It's a young country. You always feel—it's strange, you're not aware of it until you've been there—that you're looking for your roots, your culture. You see this manifested very often in different parts of the United States.

Typically, of course, in Zeeland it's the Dutch background. It's a funny thing, but very often when I talk to people from Holland—the Netherlands—who go back to the States, they speak of customs they see being reenacted very strongly in a way that perhaps is not even happening at home.

I would say that our roots are as strong here as they probably are in the United States. In a country such as ours that comes, industrially, from a very different backcloth, we place a very high priority on the attractions of Herman Miller. Those of us who joined Herman Miller did so because of the style of business that it is. If this isn't important to you, if it doesn't mean anything to you, then you're probably not in the right company.

Carl Frost

Maybe because of the continuity of leadership and modeling, there has been more consistency at Herman Miller in preserving its integrity and having it open to question. When Max became president I asked him, "Now, Max, is there a role that would be appropriate for me to play in this organization."

He said, "After thirty years you'd ask that question?"

Quite recently, I asked Max another question: "Is the perception of the continuity of leadership sensitive to the Christian quality of the company legacy?"

He said, "Personally, I would hope so."

And so I said, "Well, I guess in some ways there's a value system that is extended by that perception, and that it enables the people at Herman Miller to feel it is not inappropriate for them to believe they are a body of men and women who have a great deal in common, not just in the work place but in life."

QUALITY AND EXCELLENCE

Ann Hines
Training and Facilities Manager,
Herman Miller United Kingdom

Original member of Herman Miller's Bath group; works hard to preserve Herman Miller's history and pass it on to newcomers.

We were talking recently about training these masses of new people who are coming in. One of our managers asked, "How do we train them in the company values?"

I said, "I really don't know. I can't write it into a program, be-

cause it is something that is just absorbed. But as long as you have the right people who are setting those standards, it can be absorbed as a very automatic process."

Jacqui Peterssen
Machinist, Herman Miller United Kingdom

A skilled craftsperson; understands and perpetuates Herman Miller's idea of quality.

At the end of the day, you look at what you've done; and when you've made a chair—especially if it's a soft pad, three or four pads, you know, the leather ones—you can lay it out and think, "Ah, that's really nice." And you can feel proud of what you've done.

Stan Schrotenboer
Product Project Leader, retired

One of the original gang in the Upholstery Department; became foreman, and later assumed larger responsibilities; has never lost his spirit, openness, and blunt honesty.

One of the things that sticks with me is what D.J. told me when I was a young guy and became a supervisor here. He asked me what was my job. And I told him my job was to make sure that I meet the schedules. That we do it right.

And D.J. said to me, "What about your people?" He said, "Every decision you make"—and I had forty-one people working for me at that time—"affects forty-one families."

He said, "If you ever have to fire anybody, the first person you should look at is yourself—to see if you taught them right and did it right."

BUSINESS AS UNUSUAL

INNOVATION AND RISK

Bob Propst

We have been involved with a procession of wonderful people. And you really need them, because the outside world is ruthless about embryonic innovation. It is devastating. In its early stages, innovation is very fragile. It is toddling around. It does not know how to stand up, and it can't say anything very well. People can't understand what you are talking about. You don't have the right words together. The facts are not apparent. What are the test results? There are none.

Ed Simon

Change is incredibly difficult to implement, even in a company that advocates change. Because, in reality, there are just a few who advocate it. It's only the visionary people in a company who advocate change as a positive thing. The average person in a company does not believe that change is really that good for them—only in retrospect.

Vern Poest

Everybody always talks about the Dutch work ethic. Dutchmen work hard, you know. They work hard and save their money and buy their own houses. So they are bound to succeed because everybody works hard.

How come then if we are all Dutchmen in this whole Holland-Zeeland community, there is this Herman Miller—which is one of a kind? Why weren't all the Dutchmen like this? Why have so many of their other businesses gone by the board?

I'll tell you one important factor that makes a difference. That is the risk-taking. Because we took the risks, we got the rewards. And the rewards were much bigger and better and different than you and I would ever have imagined.

REPRISE

IMAGE AND REALITY

Glenn Walters

You can have a clarity of understanding of who you are and what you want to become, and that's essential. But implementing what you want to become, making it happen, and then running into things that may get in the way of this clarity—that's reality.

In fact, whenever I was a party to showing the corporate statement to anybody—which would include our Scanlon commitment—I would say, "Now, if you believe that is an accurate reflection of Herman Miller, I want to tell you it isn't."

There would be these gasps, and I would say, "We're not trying to mislead you. We're just trying to say that's what we'd like to become. That's our standard. It's very important that we portray that standard, that intent to achieve. We'll always fall short. In fact, that's what high standards are all about."

Charles D. Ray, M.D.
Board Member, Herman Miller

Long-time friend of Herman Miller; design consultant in the field of health care; involved with design and designers at Herman Miller.

I look at corporate growth somewhat in the way that animals with exoskeletons grow—like lizards grow. They get to a certain size and they crack. The shell cracks. Then out of this comes a new being that grows until it cracks again. These cracking processes occur at different sizes. They may occur for the first time when you've earned your first million. And then it occurs again when you're about ten million. And then about twenty-five to fifty. And then 100.

Now Herman Miller is undergoing another cracking process because of becoming a $500 million corporation. I see the corporation as managing those cracks pretty well, and I think it does so in part by swapping their managers around. That is, you don't have a man in marketing who knows nothing about design and development—and vice versa. You don't have people in manufacturing who don't understand finance. To most cor-

porate eyes, this would seem almost absurd.

I've written poetry, and I've written a poem about how difficult it is to write poetry, because I read it at another time and I don't have the same feeling for it I did at the time I wrote it. How could I expect anybody else to have the feeling when they don't know either condition?

It is a tough assignment to convey that feeling in a corporation. I think there should be a thread of homeliness in it, because in the beauty of Herman Miller lies also the heart of the home within the family and within the extended family—which is the whole working environment around us.

Following my retirement, Ralph Caplan asked me in an interview, "If you were going down for the third time and had time for one last shout to your successors, what would it be?" For an answer, I shouted, "Look for the giants! Take a chance! Trust the people!"

Now I have been retired six years. Occasionally someone phones, or I meet a former associate here or there. So I'm not completely disconnected. But 1,500 miles from Zeeland, Michigan, I have little opportunity to play the elder statesman's role. I could not do that, anyway, for it was important for me to ensure my successors their freedom from over-the-shoulder peeking, hanging around or second guessing.

But with this book, I have had my chance to offer my view of the company I led for seventeen years—to tell what happened, how things happened, and what these happenings have meant to Herman Miller. It is my chance to tell what I believe is important in this business which so many of us have shared.

Since even the musical reprise needs a concluding passage, a coda (or tail, in Italian), allow me to tail off by summing up eight ideas you have encountered in this book:

Be alert to fortuitous encounters. "How to" books on management tell us everything we need to know to become scientific managers. What they don't stress is the importance of fortuitous encounters. Life at Herman Miller has been full of them. My most critical one occurred when I went to Chicago and learned at an open plan seminar that we were not alone, that our leading edge was fading, and that we'd better move fast to complete our work on Action Office.

Be willing to risk. I learned about risk from D.J. And

when it was my risk to take, we risked the company on Robert Propst's exciting ideas. In so doing, we risked warm and fruitful relationships with Nelson and Eames, who disagreed with Propst's concepts. We risked with other projects—such as a retail residential experiment and the Textile and Objects shops—and failed. Think about it: What is the right thing to do? What is the wrong thing? Be willing to risk with the "wrong" thing.

Watch for entropy. The brim of Niagara Falls recedes year by year through the force of the water destroying the hard rock underneath, bit by bit. It is scarcely noticeable unless measured over decades. So, too, a business can be eroded by the force of a self-imposed need for more and more sales and higher profits every quarter, either to satisfy analysts or through a lack of understanding of business principles.

Tradition and lore are vital, but they can become the burdens of yesterday if allowed to level new ideas. So maintain a dynamic program by seeing in new ways. Quality and excellence are always in jeopardy. I once made a month-long, nationwide tour of dealers and installations gathering dozens of examples of below-par products and service complaints. We held a general management meeting to study and solve these problems. We committed ourselves to drive for vast improvement, and managers finally understood, accepted and passed on this drive through the organization. So watch out for entropy: It sets in before you recognize it.

Give a person a chance. Bill Stumpf was unhappy in his work as a designer at our research company. He believed he had ideas that should be developed, but he felt stifled in a research climate. We discussed the problem and worked out a solution: We would set him up in his own office, finance him for a year, and see if his ideas were valid for Herman Miller. They were, for Bill's chairs and office systems designs have provided another dimension for the business.

CODA

Many years ago, Ed Nagelkirk asked for the job of foreman. I didn't think he was able to do the job. He said, "How do you know how fast I can run until you let me go to the starting line?" He got the job and went on to become factory superintendent.

Offering people a chance not only gives them opportunity. It gives them dignity. Be a good steward of these talents.

Make someone responsible for making money. Any business that is not making a profit is a poor contributor to society and a bad investment for people's money and lives. I learned this lesson from Frank Seidman, the founder of Seidman & Seidman, one of the Big Eight in auditing and accounting. I asked him to study our business because our profits were too low, even for survival. Following a week of looking at us, he came to my office to report, "Young man, I have only one thing to tell you," he said. "Any damn fool can give it away."

D.J. admits he was a poor profit producer. I saw the critical need for profit but lacked the knowledge and ability to drive for it. Vern Poest joined us and assumed the responsibility for profit. He seldom failed to ask, "Can we afford it? Can we make money on this?"

Consider these four C's—creativity, change, contradiction and care. We open a door to creativity when we make life a program of possibilities. In the search for possibilities, with wonder and understanding that the world is different to eyes that learn how to see, life can be satisfying and exciting. Develop such a vision. Be a person of possibilities, and we will continue to be a company of creative people as far as we can see.

Change is not normal. On the contrary, it is normal for people to crush anything strange or different. So we must ally ourselves as changemakers in a select organization— reaching for the leading edge, foreseeing, seeking and striving for change.

There is an old German saying: "To avoid trouble, hang

yourself at an early age.'' Contradiction is a part of life. Contradiction is a necessity in a leading-edge, dynamic organization. We need to accept it and make it work for us.

Care has two sides. One is love and the other discipline. Love helps us to see our responsibility to others and enables us to be stewards of our talents. Such love helps to build the sense of community we need to work together. But love is not enough. We need to practice a rigorous discipline: to demand much from ourselves; to cultivate an inner urge to set standards beyond ourselves; to invent difficult assignments and force ourselves to perform them. Then we may realize the rewards of a better way of living—in the words of Goethe, ''A life of obligations, not rights.''

Keep asking questions. Who are we? Where are we going? How have we changed in the last five years? Why? What difference have I made?

Whistle while you work. I have found it is fun to examine a critical problem, arrive at a solution, assign responsibility for it—and then watch people work through it. For each of us, work must be fun. If it isn't, one should find something else to do. There must be a sense of joy, of expectation, a feeling of community and of anticipation in our work. If together we can create such a communion, we will surely whistle while we work.

From the beginning until today, we have experienced change that could not have been foreseen or even imagined. We have seen change in many, many lives—lives that were radically affected. It is this change, occurring in a climate of openness, that has been one of the differences in the particular business I have made our case study in this book. I have used this company to show that business can be more than making money, more than ''them and us,'' more than a hive of worker bees witlessly supplying the needs of the queen.

Our lives spent together at Herman Miller have differed

in details, but we have shared a common era and a common history that have given each of us a great store of common memories. And those of us with the most seniority have shared the anxiety of near bankruptcy—and then the exhilaration of a providential challenge to change from traditional to modern furniture.

We shared the frightening times of keeping a business alive with no raw materials during World War II—and then the breathtaking times opened to us by the creative energies of George Nelson and Charles Eames. Together, we have seen the need for information that would help to make us more effective, for professional financial management; and, yes, the need to earn profits that not only enabled us to survive but to grow. We set in motion the change from complete concentration on design to emphasis on marketing and sales, and we have been strengthened by the growth that came from that change. We achieved this growth, not by abandoning our faith in design but rather by complementing it with fresh organizational resources. We shared the dangers and difficulties of putting all our eggs in one basket—the chair business— and of asking our designers always to design us out of our problems.

We were warmed, as a family is warmed by good news, when we embraced the Scanlon Plan as the way to manage the company.

We were fascinated but bewildered at times by the ideas introduced by Robert Propst. And we vacillated occasionally about what to do with them. But we rejoiced together when we changed the company, when we clearly set our direction by these ideas. Then we watched each other perform in unbelievable ways to bring them—in the form of new interiors systems—to the market. And we shared astonishment at the success we had created together.

All of the events and people in this book have become part of a portrait of one organization. Herman Miller's picture is made from common memories and innumerable individual faces.

In this kaleidoscope of principles, people, events, fortuitous encounters and peak experiences, you may find the common memories we have shared, together with the details from my memory that I have sought to bequeath to those who, in the future, will be responsible for the future.

INDEX

INDEX

ગ્રાંથ ધ્રુવ ૭૯૮.૭૯.૧